LOS ANGELES REVIEW OF BOOKS QUARTERLY JOURNAL | WINTER 2014

EDITOR-IN-CHIEF / QUARTERLY EDITOR
TOM LUTZ

EXECUTIVE EDITOR
JONATHAN HAHN

SENIOR EDITORS
EVAN KINDLEY, CLARISSA ROMANO,
LAURIE WINER, KATE WOLF

POETRY EDITOR
GABRIELLE CALVOCORESSI

ART DIRECTOR
MEGAN COTTS

PUBLICATION DESIGN
ELIZABETH KNAFO

ART CONTRIBUTORS
JOHNNY HARRIS, ELIZABETH KNAFO, AMANDA ROSS-HO,
MAUREEN SELWOOD, MATT SIEGLE, DAVID SNYDER,
CLARISSA TOSSIN, JAMES WELLING

BOARD OF DIRECTORS
ALBERT LITEWKA, CHAIRMAN; BILL BENENSON,
LEO BRAUDY, BERT DEIXLER, SETH GREENLAND,
ERIC LAX, SUSAN MORSE, JON WIENER,
JAMIE WOLF, ROSANNE ZIERING

COPY EDITORS
CAROLINE BOWMAN, ANDREA GUTIERREZ,
WALTER HEYMANN, ANTAL NEVILLE

BUSINESS AND PRODUCTION
GINGER BUSWELL, C.P. HEISER, OLIVIA SMITH

SPECIAL THANKS TO
ADAM SOMERS

COVER ART
JAMES WELLING, *4559*, 2007
INK JET PRINT, 31" x 42" (78.7 x 106.7 CM)
COURTESY THE ARTIST AND REGEN PROJECTS, LOS ANGELES.

CONTENTS

Victoria Dailey — *Two Devils in the City of Angels* 4

Fady Joudah — *The Scream* 23

Bruce Robbins — *Love Fest* 24

Sarah Blake — *20. 33. 40.* 31

Annalisa Quinn — *A Visit with Mary Beard* 32

Daniel Olivas — *Two Questions for Juan Felipe Herrera* 36

Geoff Nicholson — *Voyages Around the Room* 38

Francesca Lia Block — *Signs of Life* 45

Michael Wood — *The Sartre Scenario* 46

Michael Robbins — *Oh Wow* 51

Dinah Lenney — *Cell Phone Diaries* 52

Leo Braudy — *Crowd Control* 57

Colin Dickey — *The Known World* 58

Artist Portfolio: James Welling 66

George Prochnik — *Lucien and Sigmund: Thinking in Pictures* 78

Lauren K. Alleyne — *Post-Verdict Renga for Trayvon* 91

Jack Pendarvis — *Work, Encouragement, Travel* 93

M.P. Ritger — *Translations from the Bone House: On the Poetry of Seamus Heaney and John Hollander* 94

Susan Straight — *Now the Green Blade Riseth* 107

Alice Bolin — *There There* 108

Laila Lalami — *The Chronicles of the Veil* 114

John Rechy — *Say They're Pretty: On Fictional Characters and Real Life* 118

FACING PAGE: DAVID SNYDER, *WALL*, 2013

THE PUNISHMENT CELL BLOCK ON ST. JOSEPH BY ROBERT NILES, JR. FROM *CONDEMNED TO DEVIL'S ISLAND* BY BLAIR NILES, 1928.

TWO DEVILS IN
THE CITY OF ANGELS

VICTORIA DAILEY

IN THREE PARTS

"Ah, Gentlemen, you are come into a tomb!"
— J.P. Ramel, *Narrative of the Deportation to Cayenne*, 1799

"'Like California?' she laughed at the idea that anyone might not like it.
'Why, it's a paradise on earth!'"
— Nathanael West, *The Day of the Locust*, 1939

INTRODUCTION

The extremes of postmortem geography were obviously on the minds of 18th-century colonists when they named one settlement for heaven and another for hell: Los Angeles and Devil's Island.

El Pueblo de la Reina de Los Angeles — The Village of the Queen of the Angels — was a tiny, remote outpost of the Spanish Empire founded in 1781 to supply various military forts in the vicinity with cattle and farm products. Felipe de Neve, the Spanish governor of the Californias, was responsible for the name — a big one, fanciful even, for an emerging adobe village of 44 men, women, and children who had trekked here from Sonora and Sinaloa.

Spanish for 40 years and Mexican for over two decades after 1821, the dusty pueblo on the banks of the Los Angeles River became American in 1848 — it was part of the territory of California that the United States acquired after the Mexican War. Its population had grown to around 2,000, and with its new allegiance to the United States and the American belief in progress, Los Angeles began an unprecedented period of growth. In its first six decades, the City of Angels went from being a frontier outpost at the northern, neglected edge of the crumbling Spanish Empire to an expanding city on the western edge of the thriving American one.

Eighteen years before Los Angeles was founded — in another distant corner of the New World — a different empire bestowed a similarly Christian-inspired name on one of its possessions: *Île du Diable*, Devil's Island, so named in 1763. The tiny isle with the infernal name is located nine miles off the coast of French Guiana in South America — one of three coastal islets that were once known as the Triangle Islands. French colonial governor Jean-Baptiste Thibault de Chanvalon renamed them *Îles du Salut* (Salvation Islands), hoping these specks of land just off the coast were free of the tropical diseases that were decimating the mainland's colonizers. They didn't — a better name would have been the Damnation Islands. Chanvalon named the other two islands *Île Royale*, after the reigning King Louis XV, and *St. Joseph*, in honor of the saint under whose protection his expedition set out. In choosing the name *Île du Diable*, Chanvalon not only transcribed the local Kali'na Indians' name for the rocky, barren islet — they believed it was the home of an evil spirit — but also took note of the hazardous, shark-infested currents and pounding waves that battered the island.

Although the name was apt, Chanvalon would have been astonished that within 35 years, it would prove prophetic — and within 100, it could not have seemed more literal. It would soon become one of the most reviled places on earth — yet for a place so infamous, Devil's Island is small, just 36 acres. (St. Joseph is slightly larger at 50 acres, while Île Royale is 69 acres.)

It would seem that the City of Angels and the Island of the Devil have only an etymological link, a consequence of 18th century cognomination. But as a result of the French Revolution, a connection was forged that has been, until now, overlooked. Los Angeles became the home of the two most illustrious men to have ever escaped Devil's Island — Charles De Rudio in the 19th century and René Belbenoit in the 20th —and their stories of war, imprisonment, torture, survival, and eventually, fame in books and film, are so extraordinary as to defy belief. They are the central players in a true adventure that binds these two places, creating a little known, but direct tandem between the idyllic pueblo in Southern California named after heaven, and the horrific French prison colony named after hell.

PART I

The Damnation Islands

Although many are familiar with the name "Devil's Island," few can locate it, and fewer still are aware of its abject history. It is one of those places that has crept into the popular imagination without having many facts attached to it, like Transylvania, Timbuktu, or Siberia.

Despite being little known, Guiana has a long history. A century after Columbus first visited it in 1498, Sir Walter Raleigh sailed in, convinced that the fabled city of El Dorado was somewhere in the Guianan jungle. Like all the other colonizers mad with dreams of gold, he never found it, but the account of his voyage, published in 1596, was influential. The region was settled, on and off, by various European powers in the 17th century. France won ultimate possession of the eastern section in 1667. The British got the western portion while the Dutch took the middle.

But French colonization of the New World did not go as well as other European overseas conquests, and by the mid-18th century, France, having lost its Canadian territories and part of Louisiana, was left with several Caribbean islands, including Guadeloupe and Martinique, and, a thousand miles to the southeast, Guiana. As a last ditch effort to create a successful mainland colony, the French government encouraged 12,000 of its citizens in 1763 to settle in French Guiana under the leadership of Chanvalon. Within two years, 10,000 of them had perished from yellow fever, dysentery, and other tropical diseases. Chanvalon's venture has been called "the most abysmal failure, in terms of lives lost, in the annals of American colonization." (J. R. McNeill, *Mosquito Empires*, 2010.) The jungle was unforgiving. The equatorial climate, unvaryingly hot and humid, is accompanied by rainfall of 100 inches per year, making inland farming difficult, while the coastal soil, salty and sulfurous, could not be cultivated. Located between 2 and 6 degrees north latitude, French Guiana is in the Doldrums, a constant threat to ships, and hence, commerce; there were no natural harbors, on top of which the muddy beaches were clogged by mangroves; countless insects, spiders, and snakes made life miserable, if not deadly, for Europeans.

But then, as if Satan himself ordained it, the French Revolution changed French Guiana from a failed agrarian experiment into a laboratory for state-sponsored punishment and brutality. Devil's Island, true to its name, would become Hell.

By 1792, France was in chaos. The revolutionary movement had become overwhelmed by competing ideologies and the task of crushing its enemies; capital punishment was written into the nation's new set of laws. Being products of the Enlightenment, the members of the Assembly supported a recent invention to make death less painful and quicker than the traditional methods of drawing-and-quartering or the wheel: the guillotine. It was first tested on April 25, 1792, with a highway robber, and by the end of the revolution, up to 40,000 criminals and enemies of the state had lost their heads to the "national razor." (The guillotine proved efficient; it was in use until 1977.) But this was not the only form of punishment the revolution meted out. In 1793, facing the growing problem of Catholic priests who would not swear loyalty to the revolution, the Assembly passed a law providing for the deportation to French Guiana of those priests and lay brothers who would not swear an oath to maintain liberty

and equality. (Their oath was to God.) This banishment to the tropics, which usually resulted in death, albeit a slow one, became known as the "dry guillotine," and in 1795, the newly developing prison colony in the jungles of Guiana received its first inmates, both priests and enemies of the revolution.

At first, the political prisoners were granted some degree of liberty — they were

DE RUDIO IN 1875 IN HIS ARMY DRESS UNIFORM

allowed to live freely in Cayenne, the capital, as did Jean-Marie Collot d'Herbois, an actor, publisher and revolutionary legislator who had saved the life of Madame Tussaud. (She had been imprisoned as a royalist for having made wax likenesses of Louis XVI and his family, and was sentenced to the guillotine in 1793. Through the efforts of Collot, who was a member of the ruling Committee of Public Safety, Madame Tussaud was released, able to

VIEW INSIDE ONE OF THE DEVIL'S ISLAND PRISON DORMITORIES BY ROBERT NILES, JR.
FROM *CONDEMNED TO DEVIL'S ISLAND* BY BLAIR NILES, 1928.

continue her career as a wax artist.) The freedom to move about the capital was short-lived, and a primitive prison was soon set up along the Sinnamary River about 50 miles west of Cayenne. The settlement at Sinnamary was nothing more than a few huts, a deteriorating church that had been used as a prison for fugitive slaves, and a fort manned by 80 soldiers and guards.

General Jean-Pierre Ramel, despite being a revolutionary war hero, was suspected of royalist views and sentenced to deportation in 1797. He arrived at the Sinnamary prison, along with 14 other political prisoners, in November 1797 and recalled:

> It now remains for me to portray the refinement of cruelty with which, even in this prison, our persecutors harassed the miserable remnant of our existence; the insatiable rage of our executioners; the patience and constancy of their victims; the agonies of those of our companions who died in our arms […] Our only food was an allowance of biscuit, a pound of salt meat, and a glass of rum, to correct the extreme bad quality of the water. Sometimes we had bread that we could not eat, because it was full of worms and ants.

The abuse of prisoners thus originated in the colony's earliest period; it does not come as a surprise that for most of the 1790s, the governor of French Guiana was Nicholas Jeannet, the nephew of Georges Danton, one of the revolution's seminal figures and a leader during the Reign of Terror. Ramel, in his memoir, theorizes that Jeannet wanted to appear as strong — and brutal — as possible in order to impress his uncle, whom he assumed would remain in power for years to come. He was wrong. Danton was guillotined in April 1794. (Madame Tussaud cast his head in wax.)

Under Jeannet's regime, which set the precedent for the following ones, prisoners were fed rotten food, and very little of it. Insects and snakes shared their filthy cells that were furnished with nothing but hammocks. Ramel recalled: "No European, perhaps, had ever before been thrown into such a den, in such a climate, there to be given as prey to scorpions, millipedes, gnats, mosquitoes, and many other species of insects, equally numerous, dangerous, and disgusting! We were not even secure from the serpents that frequently crept into the fort." His description of the surrounding country is equally hair-raising:

> All I saw from the ramparts of our prison was a vast, and apparently impenetrable forest. The mournful howlings of tigers that came within musket shot of the fort, the shrill and piercing screams of monkeys, the discordant notes of parrots, and the croaking of venomous toads, of which the fosses and the muddy banks of the river were full, rendered this scene a wilderness of horror.

A "wilderness of horror" indeed. Apart from being nearly starved and forced to live under debilitating conditions, the prisoners also had their speech restricted. They were forbidden to discuss the subject of slavery, and should a prisoner show pity for the African slaves who worked at the prison, he was to be shot instantly. Like slaves, prisoners were often kept in irons, and although slavery had been officially outlawed by the revolution in 1794, the ban was easily ignored through double-talk and various legal maneuvers. Jeannet also confiscated all of the prisoners' letters, both those they had written and those they received. Subjected to such treatment, prisoners dream only of one thing — escape — and Ramel has the distinction of being among the first to successfully escape from Devil's Island.

By the spring of 1798, over half of Ramel's fellow prisoners had died. He, along with a few of the survivors, determined to make a getaway, and with the help of an American sea captain, managed to elude their torturers and flee to neighboring Suriname and from there, to London. Ramel received permission to return to France where he again fought in the army with distinction, becoming a major general. After the defeat of Napoleon and with the restoration of the Bourbon monarchy, Ramel became a suspect; this time, he was thought to hold revolutionary sympathies and was assassinated by reactionaries in 1815. He had survived Guiana, but not the revolution. His memoir, published in 1799, is the first to document the horrors of the prison colony.

—m—

During the revolution, the political culmination of the Enlightenment, the French became so addicted to rationality they attempted to reorganize not just society, but time itself. Completely abandoning the past, the revolutionaries adopted a new calendar based on a decimal system. The new order began when 1792 became Year I. (In imitation of the Roman Republic, the years were written in Roman numerals.) The French jettisoned the past, and dispensing with the Gregorian calendar, arranged the year into a "rational" system based on multiples of 10. Each of the newly named months (Thermidor, Fructidor, Floréal, etc.) was made up of three 10-day weeks. Each day was divided into 10 hours made up of 100 minutes. Each minute had 100 seconds. The entire metric system in use today — meters, centimeters, millimeters, grams, kilograms, and liters — originated in the revolution. While this rational system of weights and measures succeeded, the calendar failed. Who wants to work nine days a week, and not many a man could last for a 100-minute hour, even if he was French. [*Sixty-Minute Man*, http://www.youtube.com/watch?v=OpQuNY3XFI0] Napoleon ordered a return to the Gregorian system beginning on January 1, 1806, when practicality overcame reason.

French Guiana, where the rational rarely found a home — and where the jungle, like time, proved untamable — faded from the world's view after its brief notoriety as a prison colony during the revolution. By 1832, the colony's population was nearly 23,000 — of which 19,000 were slaves. Although the Revolution had abolished slavery during Year II (1794), Napoleon reinstated it in Year X (1802) when, again, the efficient defeated the rational. Napoleon recognized that the country's sweet tooth could not be satisfied without more sugar, and that more sugar and huge profits were only possible with slave labor. It was only logical. (Slavery was legal in France until 1848.) Yet despite the attempts to successfully cultivate sugar in French Guiana, the colony only produced about 2 percent of France's supply during the 19th century. It was a difficult place.

By mid-century, Napoleon III faced strong opposition from many sides after he assumed his emperorship; he needed a place to send political enemies and criminals since the prisons and convict hulks that were regularly used to house prisoners were overcrowded. France's overseas sugar plantations were also suffering from the lack of labor caused by the recent abolition of slavery. The emperor hit upon an ominous solution: reopening and expanding the deteriorating prison settlements in French Guiana, where convicts could be forced to work on plantations, taking the place of slaves. He may have been influenced by the success of the British system of deporting criminals to Australia, which had begun in 1786, but there was one crucial difference: climate. A sentence of deportation to Australia did not usually end in death as it did in French Guiana. In addition, hundreds of thousands of immigrants willingly settled in Australia where they created a successful country. Very few people ever went to French Guiana voluntarily.

However he came up with the idea, Napoleon III took action. On May 11, 1852, the first shipload of 298 convicts reached the jungle colony. By 1870, nearly 20,000 would arrive at that fatal shore, and by the time it was closed in 1953, Devil's Island had received about 80,000 convicts. Because of the high mortality rate, only a few thousand prisoners were ever detained there at any one time. Escape was virtually impossible. The jungle, with its multitude of problems, was a natural barrier: disease, insects, wild animals, uncrossable rivers, intense heat, and native populations who were paid to capture and return any escapees they might encounter, prevented its use as an escape route. The only other alternative, the Atlantic Ocean, also posed an obstacle — not only were its currents dangerous to the type of small boat or raft a prisoner might obtain, but patrol ships were on constant duty.

As a result, only a handful of men ever escaped from Devil's Island once it reopened in 1852, and of those, two became illustrious, surviving experiences so extreme that they defy belief. (Papillion, the well-known account of Henri Charrière published in 1970, is now considered to be an amalgamation of stories the author heard while a prisoner on Devil's Island, not an actual account of his own experiences. Alfred Dreyfus, the island's other celebrated prisoner, spent the years 1895–1899 there in solitary confinement and was not an escapee.) But there are two men, Charles De Rudio in the 19th century and René Belbenoit in the 20th, who each made the figurative journey from hell to heaven — and the actual one from Devil's Island to Los Angeles. Their epic stories could not be more metaphoric, not to mention the infinitesimal odds that the colony's two most renowned escapees would each end up in Los Angeles — two "devils" in the City of Angels.

PART II
The First Devil: Charles De Rudio

"The real purpose of the state is to increase by a hundred all the means possible to corrupt its subjects."
— Marquis de Sade, *Juliette*

Although the French had reverted back to monarchy, revolutionary movements were springing up all over Europe in the 19th century. In France, Napoleon III was especially loathed by Giuseppe Mazzini and the Italian freedom fighters — the Carbonari — who were seeking to overthrow their Austrian rulers, unite Italy, and overturn the power of the Pope. To appease French Catholics, the emperor had sent troops to Italy in support of the Pope, and enraged by this action, several Italian insurgents hatched a plot to assassinate the emperor. On January 14, 1858, they threw three bombs at the emperor's carriage as he arrived at the opera in Paris. He escaped with a bloody nose, but eight bystanders were killed, as were several horses, and 142 people were wounded. Unbeknownst to the perpetrators, they had been under police surveillance and were quickly arrested. The would-be assassins included Carbonari members Felice Orsini, Giuseppe Pieri, Antonio Gomez, and lastly, Carlo De Rudio, an Italian nobleman and soldier whose life story is among the 19th century's most astonishing in a field crowded with incredible biographies.

The life of Charles De Rudio is improbable and remarkable — as thrilling, and in many ways parallel, to the fictional life of Edmond Dantès, the hero of Dumas' *The Count of Monte Cristo*. De Rudio was born into an impoverished aristocratic family in the small northern Italian town of Belluno, 50 miles north of Venice and then part of the Austrian Empire.

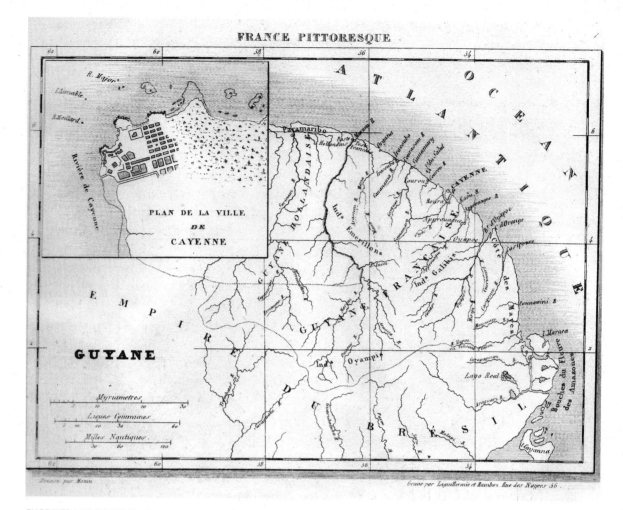

ENGRAVED MAP OF FRENCH GUYANA FROM *FRANCE PITTORESQUE*, PARIS, 1835.

Becoming a soldier was his only real career choice; he entered the Austrian army as a cadet in 1845. When Italian insurgents stormed the academy where he was in training during the upheavals of 1848, De Rudio refused to fight against his own countrymen and was imprisoned, the first of many incarcerations and the beginning of his decade-long life as a revolutionary.

Released after a short time, he joined the insurgents, was captured, and was again sent to prison — but this time he escaped, ultimately finding his way to Rome in 1849 where he joined Garibaldi's forces fighting the French army. After numerous skirmishes, brushes with death and prison escapes, De Rudio arrived in Paris in November 1851 just as Louis-Napoleon was staging the coup d'état that resulted in his becoming Emperor Napoleon III. For four days De Rudio fought alongside the losing resistance forces, then escaped to Switzerland. Setting out in a snowstorm, he hiked alone across the Alps into Italy, managing to get to Turin where he had comrades in the ongoing insurgency against the Austrian government. Assigned the task of becoming a spy, he was issued a false passport so that he could travel to various towns in northern Italy to obtain information on troop movements.

In Genoa in early 1853, he was entrusted with carrying 4,000 gold lire to insurgents at

Intra on the western shore of Lake Maggiore who were planning to attack Milan. Before the plan could unfold, police, alerted by informants, rushed inside the inn where De Rudio was staying. He jumped out a window, climbed over a garden wall and made it down to the lake, the police in hot pursuit. De Rudio jumped into a rowboat and, at gunpoint, ordered the astonished oarsmen to take him across the lake to Locarno, Switzerland, 20 miles away. Naturally, it was a dark and stormy night, and they had to make for shore before reaching their destination. De Rudio still paid the boatmen, then made his own way to Locarno on foot, where he rejoined the other conspirators. Forced to call off their upcoming attack, they sent De Rudio to Lugano to deliver the gold directly to Mazzini. He completed this task, but was again arrested by Swiss police, and facing a judge, was sentenced to deportation. He was given a choice of going to the United States or England. He chose England, a hotbed of the Carbonari.

De Rudio arrived in London in April 1853 but soon returned to Switzerland where he learned that the Carbonari were going to attack Belluno, his own home town. He then set out alone for Belluno on another arduous trek through the Alps, and upon reaching the town, found an old family friend, a local priest, who informed him that the police, again tipped off, were looking for him. He escaped back into the mountains, then made it to the nearby town of Bolzano, where he saw a printed poster advertising a reward of 6,000 lire for the capture of Carlo De Rudio, dead or alive.

De Rudio fled again, to Zurich and Paris, but ignoring the danger, soon returned to Switzerland to take part in another plot. Betrayed, De Rudio was arrested and spent several months in jail before being brought to court where, for a second time, he was sentenced to deportation. He went back to England and the versatile De Rudio was able to find work in London, both in the chorus of an Italian opera company and on the docks as a laborer. He lodged at the home of an Anglo-Italian couple and began giving Italian lessons to the couple's niece, Eliza Booth, a teenage girl from Nottingham. De Rudio fell in love with the young girl, and they were married on December 9, 1855. He was just 23, his bride, 14.

After several other adventures, including surviving being stabbed, De Rudio and Eliza moved to Nottingham, where he found work as an Italian teacher and where the young couple celebrated the birth of their son Hercules in 1857. De Rudio soon moved back to London where Carbonari members were devising new plans. Led by Felice Orsini, the plotters decided to assassinate Napoleon III, and they spent the winter of 1857 making bombs and organizing the details of their plan, which they carried out on January 14, 1858. They failed, and all the conspirators were quickly arrested.

The two-day trial ended with a verdict on February 26: death by guillotine for Orsini, Pieri, and De Rudio. For cooperating with the prosecution, Gomez was sentenced to life in prison. News of the assassination attempt and the resulting trial spread around the world, and the name "De Rudio" became both reviled and celebrated, depending on one's views of emperors.

Eliza De Rudio worked feverishly to gain support for her husband's appeal. Queen Victoria became involved, as did Empress Eugénie, who had survived the assassination attempt along with her husband. The empress, also the mother of a young son, requested leniency for De Rudio, but appeals to her husband failed. Construction of the guillotine's platform began on March 11 outside La Roquette prison in northern Paris where the conspirators were being held. The next day, Napoleon III met with his ministers to consider commuting the death sentences in order to appear merciful and boost his reputation with the public. His advisers argued against mercy. However, the Archbishop of Paris suggested a compromise: because he was the only one of the conspirators to ask for mercy, De Rudio could be spared while the other two would be executed. The final decision was up to the emperor.

On March 13, the preparations were complete. Soldiers guarded the area around the prison where thousands of spectators had come to witness the triple execution. As a heavy snow began to fall, Pieri was guillotined. De Rudio was next. As he was brought up to the platform, he made one last request: to smoke his pipe. The request was granted. As he smoked, a messenger suddenly rode up on horseback, dismounted and spoke quickly to the authorities. De Rudio was immediately led back to his cell. Orsini was then led to the guillotine and executed. The messenger had brought the news that Empress Eugénie, at the final hour, was able to convince her husband to spare De Rudio's life. De Rudio's death sentence was commuted to life in prison. Had he not requested his pipe, the messenger would have been too late. He spent the following months in prison until October 21, 1858, when he and his co-conspirator Gomez, along with 200 other convicts, boarded a ship bound for the "dry guillotine" of French Guiana: Devil's Island. A wax likeness of Orsini went on display at Madame Tussaud's.

———

Since 1852, when Napoleon III had ordered the resurrection of its Guianese penal colony, the French had built two new mainland prisons, one at Saint-Laurent-du-Maroni, on the Maroni River in the western part of the colony; the other at Montagne d'Argent, on the Oyapock River, in the east. There was also a prison in Cayenne, the capital, and the Salvation Islands housed prisoners as well — Île Royale became a general prison and St. Joseph was used for solitary confinement. At first, Devil's Island was rarely used since it was so inaccessible, but a system of ropes and pulleys was installed connecting it to St. Joseph, only 200 meters away, in order to convey supplies to the island. At the time, Devil's Island was usually reserved for very sick prisoners where they could easily be isolated and left to die. Later, it became the place to which political prisoners were banished.

The living conditions in the penal colony were brutal. Prisoners were fed very little, and the food was often rotten. They were whipped, chained, and beaten, and were at times put into pits in the blistering sun. The few clothes they were given soon became nothing more than rags, at which point prisoners often worked without any clothing. As if this wasn't enough, a scheme to inflict extra punishment was enacted into law in 1854. The French passed the law of *doublage*, which mandated that once, and if, a convict served out his sentence, he was required to remain in the colony for a period of time equal to his sentence, effectively doubling it. Because ex-convicts were not permitted to work once they were freed, they typically had to resort to crime just to stay alive, and, easy prey, they were caught and returned to prison. But if the sentence was eight years or more, the convict was required to remain in the colony for life. It was as if the French government had turned to sadism, enacting scenarios found in the fiction of the Marquis de Sade.

De Rudio and Gomez arrived into this abyss in December 1858 and were sent to the prison at Montagne d'Argent, a particularly swamp-like environment. They were assigned to hard labor felling trees, but in the fetid surroundings, this pursuit was more of a punishment than a purposeful task — very few roads were ever built once the trees were cleared. Of the infamous Route 1, the road connecting Cayenne to St. Laurent, it was said that one convict died for every yard completed — and by the mid-1930s, only 15 miles had been built. (The 220-mile road across the country was finally finished in 2004.)

Not one to stay in prison for long, De Rudio immediately devised an escape plan and got nine other men to join him. At night, they would sneak back into the jungle, where they hollowed out a tree trunk in order to make a large canoe that they planned to sail to Brazil and freedom. They were nearly ready to flee when some of the convicts came down with yellow fever, including all nine members of De Rudio's crew. Of the 600 prisoners and guards at Montagne d'Argent, only 63 survived the outbreak. One was De Rudio, another was Gomez.

Gomez was then sent to another mainland prison; De Rudio never saw him again. De Rudio was imprisoned on Île Royale, where he learned from other prisoners that although there had been attempts, no one had ever successfully escaped from the islands. Even if a rudimentary boat could be obtained, the sea was too rough, the sharks too numerous, the nearby ships and gunboats too vigilant, not to mention the impossibility of packing food rations, especially considering the near-starvation diet the prisoners were subjected to. And no one had money to bribe the unscrupulous guards. Above all, a skilled navigator would be required. None of these problems phased De Rudio. He immediately set out to find what was needed, and had the luck to know another prisoner, a former vicar convicted of murder, who was hiding 20,000 francs in his bible. The vicar was willing to provide the money to buy food and supplies from corrupt guards in exchange for a spot in the escape boat. Another convict, a former mariner with navigation skills, agreed to join the plot, as did a former tailor, who was able to stitch together enough canvas to make a sail.

It was December 1859. De Rudio and his men were ready to go, but at the last minute, two had to be left behind: the sail maker was sick with a fever, and the vicar, whose bible full of money would have been more valuable to most of his cohorts than his life, couldn't take the risk. The remaining men carried their provisions to the beach and hid while one of them signaled to some fisherman that he wanted to buy some fish. The convicts then rushed to the boat, overpowered the fishermen, and set off. They were spotted by guards in gunboats, but another conspirator had removed the oars from the boats and so a pursuit was impossible.

With Cousins, the experienced mariner at the helm, the boat headed out to the open sea where the escapees spent the next three days, managing to survive a storm, dense fog and the appearance of a Dutch ship, which ignored them. They hadn't eaten, only to discover on the third day that their food had been ruined by seawater. Forced to alter their course, they headed for the nearest landfall where they hoped to find food, but upon landing, and before they could find anything to eat, they discovered from some local men that they were in Dutch Guiana. This was an extremely dangerous place to have landed as the Dutch had a policy of sending back escaped convicts to French Guiana, where they faced severe punishment. They jumped back into the boat, still starving but free, hoping to make it to British Guiana where they expected sympathetic treatment. For several more days they continued their voyage until the boat became trapped in a mud shoal during low tide. Cousins ordered the men to jump overboard and lift the boat out of the mud, which they did, holding it above the mud for hours under the scorching sun until the tide came in. They put out to sea once again.

For two days they sailed onwards, hoping to reach British Guiana, when suddenly a ship flying a British flag intercepted them. The ship's captain inquired who they were and where they had come from — he was more than shocked to learn that this pitiful group of men had traveled nearly a thousand miles in a beat-up fishing dinghy without having eaten. But they were safe, near the port of New Amsterdam in British Guiana. The captain gave them food and water, and revived, the convicts headed into New Amsterdam, where they were met by the governor of the colony who thought they must be survivors of a shipwreck. They were given clean clothes and served a large meal.

Upon learning that the men were escaped convicts, the governor told them that Britain honored asylum seekers and that all they had to do was promise to work. When De Rudio announced who he was and that he was a soldier, the governor reacted in disbelief, stating that Count De Rudio had died of yellow fever while in prison. Newspapers around the world had reported on it, and De Rudio's celebrity was such that even the *Los Angeles Star* carried a small, though inaccurate, notice about him in 1860, reporting, "Rudio, one of the accomplices of Orsini in the attempt on the life of Napoleon III, died lately in Brazil, to which country he had escaped from the penal colony of Cayenne." Even Eliza thought her husband had perished after reading a similar account in an English newspaper.

De Rudio was offered lodging by the town physician who also happened to be a correspondent for the *London Times*, and on his first evening at the house, De Rudio was told that a French warship had arrived in the port in search of the escaped convicts. The French captain was demanding that the governor surrender De Rudio to him, but the governor refused, stating that the English did not grant extradition for political prisoners — De Rudio was safe for the moment. The other escapees, who all had criminal convictions, boarded a ship bound for Venezuela that same night.

Sympathetic to De Rudio's plight, the governor and the doctor vowed to help him return to England. The doctor's job as a correspondent proved extremely helpful — he sent in a false story to the *Times* reporting that the escapee De Rudio had been massacred by natives while searching for gold. This would deter potential pursuers. The governor then arranged for De Rudio's passage on an English merchant ship bound for London, and on Christmas Eve, 1859, he embarked, reaching London on February 29, 1860. He went immediately to the *London Times* to report that he was indeed alive, and then, to the home of a friend, where, in another twist of fate, Eliza arrived within moments, thinking that their friend might have updated news of De Rudio. Instead, she was greeted by him.

⁓

De Rudio began giving lectures about his experiences, but they were not well attended and he was forced to take a job in a stone factory. The couple were barely managing, and things looked bleak until De Rudio met again with Mazzini, who urged the fearless young man to go to the United States and fight for the North in the Civil War. His experiences in combat would be an asset, and as he had no others, he left for America, arriving in New York on February 22, 1864.

Mazzini had provided De Rudio with letters of introduction, and so armed, De Rudio visited Horace Greeley, editor of the *New York Tribune*. Americans generally supported the Risorgimento — the movement to create a unified, democratic Italy — and Greeley must have been impressed by this leading figure in the campaign. He sent letters to various officials to try to get De Rudio a commission in the army, but by this point, late in the war, commissions were difficult to obtain. Instead, De Rudio enlisted as a private in a volunteer infantry regiment, signing in on August 25th, 1864 as Charles De Rudio — he used this Anglicized version of his name for the rest of his life. He saw combat during the siege of Petersburg in Virginia, after which he was able to get a commission as a second lieutenant in the 2nd United States Colored Troops in the fall of 1864. (Commissions were easier to obtain in the newly created regiments of black soldiers.) He joined his regiment in Florida. Eliza and Hercules arrived shortly thereafter.

After the war, De Rudio worked as a civilian clerk, becoming a United States citizen in January 1866. The following year he received his coveted commission, as a second lieutenant in the army, but, as with many events in De Rudio's life, he faced a setback. It came in the form of a medical examination. The examining doctor stated that De Rudio was disqualified from the army due to a "retraction of the right testicle." It seems that after all he had been through, De Rudio didn't have the balls to be an officer in the United States Army.

Perhaps it was a ruse to keep the former revolutionary out of the American military once the war was over. Someone in the military may have learned about De Rudio's role as a bomb-thrower and wondered if he might try something similar again, especially so soon after Lincoln's assassination. But De Rudio, whose determination had seen him through worse calamities, did not give up. He consulted his own doctor, who wrote that "there is not the slightest deviation either in the shape, size or direction of the right testicle, which would in the least interfere whether in marching on foot, or horseback, nor in any posture [...] and there is not even the slightest probability that it will ever incommode him during the remainder of his life." A second doctor agreed, and De Rudio requested a reexamination by the army. He passed. And as proof of the viability of his testicles, Eliza gave birth to their daughter Roma Elisabetta two weeks later.

Another daughter, Italia Luigia, was born in 1869. That same year De Rudio was assigned to the newly formed 7th Cavalry stationed at Fort Riley, Kansas, under the command of Lieutenant Colonel George Armstrong Custer. The 7th Cavalry's assignment was to patrol the prairies in order to subdue and, if necessary, fight against native tribes who were attempting to hold onto their ancestral lands. The thousands of settlers migrating west after the civil war, seeking fresh opportunities, claimed the open territory as their own, and they wanted army protection from the people fighting to remain on that land.

De Rudio, used to following orders, was known as a diligent, hardworking soldier. He didn't drink or gamble and he was a family man. In 1872, Eliza gave birth to a third daughter, America Carlotta, and the following year, the 7th Cavalry was ordered to the Dakota Territory where the Lakota Sioux were attacking both the Northern Pacific Railroad and gold prospectors in the Black Hills.

At the end of 1875, De Rudio was promoted to first lieutenant; Custer assigned him to join a battalion commanded by Major Marcus Reno, one of four battalions under Custer's command. Custer, who had taken a dislike to the Italian count, purposely kept him out of his own battalion. De Rudio was a popular, soft-spoken raconteur with European manners, and he must have irritated the aggressive and vain Custer whose nicknames included "Iron Butt" and "Hard Ass." But with De Rudio's usual luck, Custer's dislike saved his life. Having escaped the guillotine by seconds and having survived the dry guillotine and the Civil War, De Rudio was about to participate in one of the most notorious battles in American history: The Battle of the Little Bighorn, also known as Custer's Last Stand.

In the spring of 1876, after several successful battles in the Black Hills of the Dakota Territory, Lakota, Arapaho, and Northern Cheyenne tribes had gathered in eastern Montana near the Little Bighorn River under the leadership of Sitting Bull in order to plan their next move. They were prepared to continue their fight against the army's attempt to drive them onto reservations and had assembled in large numbers — their encampment has been estimated at upwards of 7,000 men, women, and children.

Custer, planning a three-pronged attack on the encampment, divided the 7th Cavalry into three battalions led by Major Reno, Captain Frederick Benteen, and himself. The attack began during the afternoon of June 25, 1876. Custer had ignored reports about the size of the encampment, and ordered Major Reno, with 175 men, to attack the village from the south, promising support in case of trouble. The attack came as a surprise to the Indians, and many started to flee, but just as his soldiers got close to the camp, Reno ordered his troops to dismount and form a skirmish line. His reasons have never been understood, for had they continued on horseback, the soldiers would surely have been victorious. By dismounting, Reno's men gave hundreds of Indian warriors time to mount their own horses and begin a vigorous defense — they forced Reno and his troops to retreat. Within an hour, 40 of his men were dead; 37 were missing. In disarray, Reno and the survivors were able to reach a ridge, later called Reno's Hill, where Benteen and his men joined them. Custer, with his battalion of 215 men, was at vantage point several miles away, and although he had witnessed Reno's retreat, he was unaware that warriors, many fresh from the battle with Reno, were gathering in a U-shaped line around his position. Surrounded, Custer and his men faced a force too large to combat. They were annihilated in less than an hour.

The other battalions, still at a distance of four miles from Custer, did not know what had happened to Custer and his men. Reno, Benteen and their troops spent the night on the hill where they came under sporadic fire. The next day they engaged in a full battle, gradually gaining the upper hand. Towards sundown, the soldiers observed the Indians moving away towards the mountains, setting fire to the grass behind them to prevent a pursuit. That night, several of the missing men, including De Rudio, made it to Reno's Hill.

During Reno's attack, De Rudio and a few men had become separated from their battalion. They were in a wooded area where they were soon discovered and attacked by a band of several hundred Sioux. Taking cover in a thicket, De Rudio came upon a small group of soldiers and two civilian aides, most of whose horses had either been shot or run away. De Rudio took command, ordering the soldiers to make their way back to Reno's position. He stayed behind with Thomas O'Neill, an army private, and the two civilians. From their hiding place, they witnessed the Lakota women scalp Custer's fallen soldiers, remove clothing from the corpses and set fire to the woods. They began to make their way back to Reno's position during the night, only to discover that they had to cross the swollen Little Bighorn River; it was too swift and deep to make a safe crossing. Suddenly, they saw several mounted warriors approaching.

The two civilians, who were on horseback, galloped off while De Rudio and O'Neill ducked into the thick bush for cover where they spent the night. At dawn, they were relieved to see cavalry soldiers across the river and shouted out for help. A barrage of bullets was the response to their cries — the soldiers were actually warriors dressed in the uniforms taken from Custer's men. They were able to crawl back into the brush, but within minutes, other warriors near their hiding spot approached, and when they were 10 yards away, De Rudio and O'Neill opened fire, killing two. The others withdrew, setting fire to the brush. De Rudio and O'Neill took refuge in a woodpile near the river where they spent another uneasy night. The next day, they were forced to remain hidden as hundreds of Indians marched by. That night, they were at last able to make their way to Reno's camp. They had survived the Little Bighorn, and on June 29, De Rudio joined the troops who went to inspect Custer's battlefield. Acting as secretary, De Rudio counted 212 corpses, including Custer's. It was a week before the nation celebrated its centennial.

De Rudio remained on duty in the Dakota Territory and was promoted to captain in 1882. From 1884–1886 he was stationed in New York and then served in Kansas, Oklahoma, Texas, and the Arizona Territory until 1895. Suffering from rheumatism, the 64-year-old De Rudio retired from the army, moving to San Diego in 1896. Two years later, the former inmate of Devil's Island settled in the paradise that was Los Angeles.

⁂

In 1898, Los Angeles was a city of nearly 103,000, known for its promising future, prosperous present and romantic past (even though most of the past had recently been invented by civic boosters). Capitalizing on the city's Spanish and Mexican heritage, which had lasted all of 67 years, urban promoters began to create an exotic image for their City of Angels in the 1890s, inaugurating a flower festival with a Spanish name: the Fiesta de Los Angeles, rechristened La Fiesta de las Flores in 1901. Los Angeles was animated with dreams of caballeros, señoritas, ranchos, and padres. Into this mix an Italian count with his own improbably heroic history of revolutionary activities, prison escapes, and epic battles fit right in. Los Angeles loved Charles De Rudio. After surviving numerous hells, where else could he have gone?

Los Angeles was the dream city of America, unlike any other in the country. Aromatic with the fragrance of orange blossoms from the thousands of orange groves dotting the landscape, as well as from countless domestic gardens filled with roses, geraniums, heliotrope, jasmine, and tuberose, the city was also awash in fanciful attractions and amusements. There was an ostrich farm where ladies could buy the fashionable feathers that adorned their hats. On the shores of the Pacific, Abbot Kinney's grandly planned and unlikely suburb of Venice attracted both settlers and tourists; it must have astonished De Rudio, who had not seen his homeland in half a century and who had grown up so close to Kinney's inspiration. After his experiences on Devil's Island, De Rudio must have looked out at Catalina, Los Angeles' own offshore island used not as a prison but as a tourist resort, as if seeing a mirage.

Another of the most popular attractions of the time was Mount Lowe, a mountain resort above Pasadena in the San Gabriel Mountains where Thaddeus Lowe had built several hotels and restaurants, including the Alpine Tavern, which, at 5,000 feet, was the highest of the resort's destinations. De Rudio, who had trekked twice through the Alps and had grown up in their shadow, could only have been amused by yet another Los Angeles version of his past. This irony was further underscored when Carlotta, De Rudio's youngest daughter, was married in 1903 at the family home on South Figueroa. Her groom, Neal Vickrey, soon became the manager of the Alpine Tavern on Mt. Lowe. De Rudio's connection to Los Angeles was sublime, and complete.

De Rudio spent 12 years in Los Angeles, more time than any other place he had lived since his childhood. His 10 years as a revolutionary were spent throughout Europe; his incarceration in French Guiana lasted a year; and he spent 30 years in the army, moving frequently. In contrast to his experiences elsewhere, De Rudio, in Los Angeles, became a renowned citizen — and a prominent member of the local Italian community. In 1909, the *Los Angeles Times* published a long article about it:

> Many Italian men who have achieved fame in various branches of the world's work have made their homes in Southern California [...] Probably the most notable of these is Maj. Charles C. De Rudio, one of Italy's greatest patriots, whose name has already been enrolled on the pages of the world's history.

De Rudio had been promoted to the rank of Major (Retired) in 1904, and his golden wedding anniversary in 1905 merited a long biographical article in the *Los Angeles Times*. In 1908 he was the guest of honor at a banquet celebrating his achievements, and as reported by the *Los Angeles Herald*:

> The man for whom the banquet was given is one of the most interesting figures of modern times [...] He was banished to Devil's Island, from which be escaped, going to London, England. From there he and his faithful wife [...] came to America.

The former "devil," who had found refuge in a town of angels, died on November 1, 1910. A generation later, another "devil" would take his place. ... CONTINUED ON PAGE 124.

DEVIL'S ISLAND AS SEEN FROM ÎLE ROYAL IN 1939.

The Scream

FADY JOUDAH

The scream that startled me while I was on my knees
depositing my son in the kindergarten line one morning in
the cafeteria/theater/gym, where he sits and waits for new
appointments and disappointments, that scream came from
behind me, from a boy with a bloody nose, his fingers bearing
the coagulating fluid of his life. I turned toward him, I the
doctor with warm sweat invading my pores, cupped his face
as if a prayer. Then a mother, not his mother, came with paper
and towel and wiped off his nose, and left as if nothing had
happened. I asked him what happened, he pointed to the boy
behind him in line. I questioned the accused but he seized
into absence. The nurse came and took Abel. I stroked Cain's
thick hair, gazed into his fixed stare. He was beautiful.

LOVE FEST

BRUCE ROBBINS

LUC FERRY, *On Love*

ALAIN BADIOU, *In Praise of Love*
TRANSLATED BY PETER BUSH

MARTHA MUSSBAUM, *Political Emotions:*
Why Love Matters for Justice

LUC BOLTANSKI, *Love and Justice as Competences*

Some people would never fall in love if they hadn't read novels.

Stendhal, riffing on La Rochefoucauld, uttered this cynical thought in a novel, and a novel containing not one but two rather compelling love stories. So you might conclude that for all his apparent cynicism he is just as much in love with love as everyone else. And you would have a case. But is that what you'd want? Consider all those people who think they can be in love without actually noticing much about the Other Person. Isn't there a side of you that doesn't mind seeing Stendhal wipe the self-satisfied smile off their faces?

If monuments were erected to literary schools, the French school of chilly moral and psychological analysis would be an excellent candidate for one. Public service was rendered when La Rochefoucauld, Constant, Stendhal and their successors, ignoring all the positive PR that passion is forever receiving, decided to focus instead on its power games, its disguised narcissism, and its other ignobilities. It took courage to suggest that love might be kindled not by someone's charms but by a novel or by the admiring gaze of someone else, perhaps a rival, in whose opinion the lover-to-be is much too interested. Obstacles had to be overcome in order for them to remind us how often love, like stalking, happens at some distance from the beloved. After all, it's a downer to have to ask, like the hero of Stendhal's *The Red and the Black* after his first night with his mistress: "is that all it is?" "N'est-ce que ça?"

For those who take pleasure in such coldbloodedness (the tradition is very much alive, though a bit less appetizing, in Michel Houellebecq), it's disconcerting to see French philosopher Luc Ferry enlist Stendhal on the other side. For Ferry, who has somewhat immodestly borrowed from Stendhal the title of his book, *On Love*, Stendhal is just another of love's many cheerleaders. What a parade Stendhal is not raining on! Ferry believes not only that love makes the world go round but that love can save the world. And to judge from the other three books under review, he's got company. It's a philosophical love fest. When the philosophers talk about love, they're so demanding.

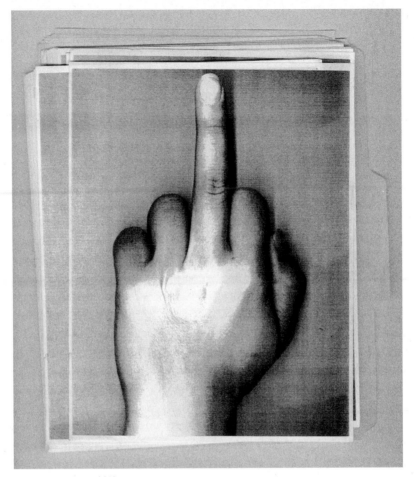

AMANDA ROSS-HO, 2010

Despite its title, Ferry's *On Love* has nothing of note to say about love. On the other hand, the book is depressingly symptomatic of the hash philosophers tend to make when they use love as the main ingredient in political arguments. What Ferry wants out of love is support for liberalism in the European sense, beginning with civilizational self-flattery. By love he means companionate marriage. Spousal choice is a proud sign of the West's unique freedoms. We freely choose whom we love, and the ones we choose are the ones we marry. That's why love and the families it founds are sacred for us — the only form of sacredness that remains to us, in Ferry's view, now that we no longer believe in God, country, or revolution. Outside Europe, on the other hand, it takes a village to make a marriage. Choices are guided by kinship and by familial economics, which means love will not express individual freedom and will not be treated as sacred. For non-Europeans, then, archaic forms of sacredness will presumably retain their ancient power. Ferry uses the contrast to display the supposed superiority of what he tenderly calls "this old Europe of ours." Ferry was the Minister of Education who in 2005 implemented France's notorious law against wearing the veil in school, and here too he seems attached to the notion that "they" submit to traditions and orthodoxies while "we" are moderns, exulting in the individuality exemplified by free erotic choice.

Like most of what Ferry has to say, his opposition between the modern West and the traditional Rest is crudely propagandistic and historically falsifiable. But you may have already thought of a different objection. Isn't the whole point about love that it seems to hit us with irresistible force, like the proverbial lightning bolt or ton of bricks? Isn't what's special about it the fact that it's not a free choice? If falling in love were like picking a brand of smartphone, would we get so worked up about it? Love is generally understood as the exception that proves the rule about liberal democracies. As Theodor Adorno writes in *Minima Moralia*: "Everywhere bourgeois society insists on the exercise of will; only love is supposed to be involuntary."

Adorno was suggesting that love is not involuntary after all: "He alone loves who who has the strength to hold fast to love." Forced to choose between love as sacred lightning bolt and love as willed choice, Adorno chooses choice. Real love for him is staying together. His position has a certain paradoxical neatness to it. Conjugal fidelity, defined by a prolonged series of small decisions, is unfreedom that is freely chosen.

This is more or less the same argument pursued by the philosopher Alain Badiou in his *In Praise of Love*. For Badiou, today's characteristic threat to love comes from internet dating-sites that sell "safe" pleasure, sexual satisfaction without emotional risk or commitment. Commodification has demystified passion. Finance capitalism's recent habits of making no commitment to its workers are reflected in the new erotic style of zero-risk relationship. That background of financially-motivated non-commitment gives love its political significance. Like Adorno, Badiou praises as real only love "that triumphs lastingly, sometimes painfully, over the hurdles erected by time, space and the world." Love overcomes the world. Fidelity is resistance.

Like Ferry, Badiou chooses the "dialogue-with-a-philosopher" format for his book, the edited version of a live performance at the Avignon Festival, and I have to say it works. *In Praise of Love* may be staged, but it feels unguarded, and it offers the unsual pleasure of intimate access to an otherwise difficult thinker. Like Ferry, Badiou seems tempted to make love a secular substitute for religion, a refuge from corrosive demystification. Otherwise, the two disagree about politics (Ferry is a figure of the right, Badiou of the left) and about almost everything else. Rather than claiming Stendhal and his fellow moralists for his side — he refers to them as "the pessimistic tradition" — Badiou takes explicit distance from them. Unlike Ferry, he rejects outright the idea that we can and should find in love guidelines for public policy. Love is like revolution (in which he believes), but he never quite says it will provide a means of arriving at one. It's good to see that love can be praised without asking quite so much of it.

At the same time Badiou's sense of the erotic is a bit dutiful. The randomness of what he calls "the encounter" sounds romantic, even sexy. But the sexiness quickly disappears from Badiou's scenario. In its essence love for him is duration, loyalty proven over time. Aside from child-rearing, the hazardous adventures are over once the knot is tied. One throw of the dice and chance is abolished forever. For Badiou, as for therapeutic discourse, love entails hard work. Laura Kipnis offers a more Stendhalian view in her *Against Love*: "Yes, we all know that Good Marriages Take Work [...] Work, work, work: given all the heavy lifting required, what's the difference between work and 'after work' again? Work/home, office/bedroom: are you ever not on the clock?"

Ferry's case that love can save the world pretty much ignores governments, parties, and movements in favor of individuals. Like many other ideologues for the present system, he assumes that you are the problem, and you are also the solution to the problem. Public actions should be defined by and limited to private interests. Love is the private interest par excellence. The demand for it is substantial and inelastic. It's the perfect commodity. Politically speaking, then, love is all you need.

Today's great political fact, Ferry argues, is that love finds *"ever greater expression in an unprecedented concern for the welfare of future generations"* (the italics are in the original). What you get if you marry for love is concern for your children — it's at this point that Ferry mentions his three daughters. Concern for your children logically takes the form of concern for the environment your children will inhabit. Hence love is the answer to the political riddle of our times. Well, concern for your children ought no doubt to express itself in this ecological and altruistic form. But this doesn't seem to be happening. Public commitment to family values as frequently goes hand in hand with the opinion that climate change is a left-wing hoax and that God can reset the earth's thermostat any time and any temperature He likes. One would like some evidence that the present is making any sacrifices at all for the future, let alone being led by familial love into generous schemes of economic redistribution. Where has familial love led? Those who can afford to will most often find an outlet for their feelings by socking away large sums for their children's future education, first car, first house, first horse, or first yacht, while the welfare of other people's children gets filed under other people's business.

Human beings may not be incurably self-interested, but love — love of the powerful, interesting, misery-inducing kind — almost certainly is. This is a strong objection to the idea of asking love to serve the cause of justice. It is spelled out, reluctantly but forcefully, in Martha Nussbaum's *Political Emotions: Why Love Matters for Justice*. As her title suggests, Nussbaum shares Ferry's interest in mobilizing love for larger ends. She also shares his impulse to cure secular liberalism's emotional anemia by giving it regular doses of the sacred — the sacred being, for her, both love and the "civil religion" of Comte and J.S. Mill. Still, Nussbaum is scrupulous enough to concede that love for spouses and families may not be up to the job. She cites Aristotle's rejoinder to Plato about why this enterprise may be a non-starter. Plato wanted citizens of his ideal city to care for all other citizens equally. Love, Aristotle answers, is partial, possessive, particularistic: "there are two things above all that make people love and care for something, the thought that it is all theirs and the thought that it is the only one they have. Neither of these will be present in that city." Even compassion, love's supposedly more enlightened and politically capable cousin, is no less vulnerable to partiality. The "vivid story" of a particular person in distress, however unrepresentative and misleading, can stir the blood to action on that person's behalf and thus "destabilize good principles" — in other words, lead to moral and political mistakes. Accounts of atrocities, whether fabricated or true, have been known to stir outrage and spur nations into wars that many years and much bloodshed later they would come to regret. In the heat of the moment, one "individual narrative of distress" seems all your heart needs to know. It's not.

This is of course a warning against depending politically on love. Nussbaum does not seem to notice that literature, to which she frequently refers, has the same problem as love, and is therefore interesting in the same way. Can a particular compassion-inducing story of atrocity be generalized? Literature appeals to her because like religion or patriotism it's able to sex up liberalism's abstractions. But she does not treat literature as capable of modifying the abstractions, only of adorning and illustrating them. A true lover of literature will worry that she doesn't feel deeply enough about it. Certainly no writer could be less literary in her own style. Nussbaum begins her definition of love as follows: "a delighted recognition of the other as valuable, special, and fascinating." The list of attributes becomes less and less fascinating, special, or valuable as it proceeds. Whole sections are cribbed from previous books as if they were precious stones that could be moved from ring to ring. There are many, many sentences of the form "we need." Nussbaum says things that are so obvious — for example, that individuality is good — that it's unclear to whom she thinks she is speaking. Who needs to be told these things? Who would disagree? In search of heroes, Nussbaum names . . . George Washington, Abraham Lincoln, Mohandas Gandhi, and Martin Luther King. This isn't going out on much of a limb. Nussbaum is not the sort of writer who, talking (as she does) about the use of fear-mongering in politics, would dare mention Hillary Clinton's 3AM phone call ad in the 2008 campaign. The writing comes alive only when she talks about the classics — for example, how the Stoic emperor Marcus Aurelius tried to cultivate distance from the emotions by reminding himself to think of "sexual intercourse" as "the rubbing together of membranes, accompanied by spasmodic ejaculation of a sticky liquid." There's also a good moment in her discussion of Comte, who apparently proposed that in his civil religion the Catholic sign of the cross might be replaced by a gesture of a different kind, a touching of the "principal organs" that would express devotion to the biological sources of life.

As Lauren Berlant has noted, the project of politicizing love always seems to come with an admixture of religion. In Love and Justice as Competences the sociologist Luc Boltanski passes over eros completely and instead spends his time on that other kind of love the Greeks called agape, which is most familiar as a name for the love between man and God. In her attempt to make love serve the cause of earthly justice, Nussbaum treats eros and agape as if they were interchangeable. Boltanski is fascinated by the difference between them. Unlike eros, he says, agape is not possessive, calculating, or self-interested. It is built entirely on the notion of the free gift without any expectation of return. It "does not rise up towards what is higher, and it does not contain the idea of desire." It has the merit of being indifferent to merit: it asks no intrusive questions, makes no requests, remembers nothing of bad behavior in the past, recognizes no debts and no limits. It refuses to measure what the beloved does or does not deserve. Justice in the usual secular sense (I didn't get my due!) is exactly what it is not about.

This foray into otherworldliness is a bit creepy, especially on the part of a sociologist. We owe sociologists much gratitude for revealing all the ways in which our erotic choices are not free but socially determined. (I think of Eva Illouz on men's hesitation to commit, or Niklas Luhmann — who quotes La Rochefoucauld — on love as a code, or Anthony Giddens, who credits Stendhal on love as a source of modern social science.) Boltanski's argument could of course be read as a sociologist's riposte to the neighboring discipline of economics: there are some things, he implies, that economic self-interest just cannot explain. For example, gift-giving. Gifts are not free, Marcel Mauss had argued. They must eventually be reciprocated; in effect, they create debts that must be repaid. (The idea that such a debt might be too great to be repaid, and thus would burden the receiver forever, was once part of Nietzsche's critique of Christianity and has now become part of Occupy's critique of student loans.) Boltanski offers a friendly and intriguing amendment: the counter-gift cannot be given right away. If a gift of equal value were to be handed instantly to the giver, the gift would in effect have been refused, the giver would have been insulted, and the social bond between them would have been broken. In other words, delay restores to the gift its quality as free, generous, excessive, sacred. Time performs a kind of miracle.

Or does it? Does the passing of time remove the equals sign between gift and counter-gift, or merely disguise it? Like Badiou on love as fidelity, Boltanski seems fascinated by the difference time makes. And again like Badiou, he seems to want love to illustrate the everydayness of anti-capitalist or non-capitalist thinking. But the evidence for agape is weaker in every sense than for eros. You can see agape at work, he says, when people hold doors open for strangers. Polite, but not more. On the other hand, I can't say I would prefer someone who goes farther in the same quasi-theological direction, like the philosopher Peter Sloterdijk. Casting about for a counter-principle to European social democracy, Sloterdijk has come up with "charity," which derives from "caritas," the Latin translation for agape. In political practice, charity would mean that Europe's 1% keep earning their bonuses in the same time-honored ways, but they cushion the destructive effects of their money making (and get to feel good about themselves) by giving some of it away afterwards. Why would this improve on the European welfare state? Because of its new, or rather old underlying principle: the aristocratic magnaminity of the rich philanthropist. I can't be the only one who finds something desperate, unhealthy, and unseemly about this groping for vintage visions in the depths of feudalism's closet. Stendhal, arch-enemy of the ancien régime, would be appalled.

Like Stendhal himself, the Stendhalians of our time are not into cynicism for its own sake. Laura Kipnis catches the spirit of Stendhal when she asks why we are forever "'freely' falling in love with mates who are also — coincidentally — good investments," but a good deal of her book might have been subtitled "Ain't no sunshine when she's gone" — as true as anything ever said on the subject of love, and as Stendhalian. In Stendhal's novels, Vivian Gornick writes in *The End of the Novel of Love*, love "provided the context within which an enormous amount could and did get said." This is no longer true. "Put romantic love at the center of a novel today, and who could be persuaded that in its pursuit the characters are going to get to something large?" That's also the point about the books of philosophy: love will not take them where they want to go, and they do love no favors by pretending it will. If you want your preconceptions shaken, go crash your car. The world needs changing, but if you want to change it, rejigging the terms of your most intimate relationship is not the place to start. Love can take you to some awesome places, but it won't take you there. Let love stories be about love. There's more than enough to talk about. ⁄⁄

ABOVE: MAUREEN SELWOOD, *SAINT JOAN*, 2012
INK AND GRAPHITE ON PAPER

20.33.40.

from *In a Wood, with Clearings, it's Spring*

SARAH BLAKE

20.

You know of a good spot to watch the sunset. Once it's dark, it's only a 10-minute walk back to the tarp.

So you get yourself there. You can see pretty far to the west. The sun is going to go down over a mountain. Another mountain.

It's not the same as watching it set over a lake—the reflection rippling up like everything's laughing—but it should be beautiful.

You can also see you have a good 20 minutes before the sky really starts to do its thing. You decide to carve your initials into a tree.

You've been carrying around a spoon you found in the bear bag, and you find a nice flat rock.

First you scoop the bark off in chunks. Then you clear the area completely by scraping the spoon over it, again and again. It's not a bad sound like some scraping.

Now you put the end of the spoon against the trunk, knock the other end with the rock, and you make a small mark.

You make a lot of small marks. You turn around and the sky is bright pink.

You're glad the sun is going to spend time every day shining on you. This version of you that will outlast your body.

If you knew how to better represent yourself than with two crap-carved letters, well Jesus, you would do that.

33.

If you tell a bird that a heart is like a bird without wings, she will tell you it is broken because it doesn't have wings.

Back under the tarp you dry off as best you can and get back in your clothes. You feel warm and for a second you mistake that for all the happiness in the world.

The mouse breaks through the dirt near your feet. Maybe she can teach you to be pleased with the small dark space under the tarp.

You sit down and hold your hand out to her. She crawls up, up to your elbow and back down. She looks at you.

How is it every animal understands an invitation?

You start to tell her about your day. You warn her the bird is coming in case something like that would startle her. When you're done talking, you lower your hand.

Before she scurries off, she nips you hard beneath your thumb. She wants to remind you she is a wild thing.

40.

The last dream is overly specific.

You are a baby wolf taken in by a horse who has recently miscarried. She nurses you. She fears you will never love her as much as she loves you.

You have the same fear. You have a wolf's howl.

You shouldn't understand abandonment but you do.

Her coat of fur is black and yours is gray. You feel as if she is the night sky and you are a cloud and together you're obscuring something like the moon. And that's good.

It feels very good to know what kind of light you can hold between the two of you.

The horse lets you lie beside her and you forget everything you're supposed to forget.

It feels like the last dream you'll ever have.

A VISIT WITH MARY BEARD

ANNALISA QUINN

The classicist Mary Beard walked into the lobby of her hotel in Washington, DC looking thoroughly windswept, though it was a windless day. A Cambridge classics professor, she's become famous in England for her BBC documentaries about the Romans, and, more recently, her outspokenness about misogynist abuse on Twitter.

For some women, Mary Beard's messy gray hair has taken on the same significance as Elizabeth Bennet's muddy petticoat or Frida Kahlo's untamed eyebrows — they seem to say, *I have much better things to worry about.* Indeed, it is impossible to have perfect hair if you do as much wild gesturing, pensive head-rubbing, and general jumping around as Mary Beard seems to do.

On her TV programs, she is excitable and perpetually disheveled, hopping around Rome in gold high-tops, pausing every so often to squat down in the dirt next to some ancient artifact or another. She sits — fully clothed and pleased as a pumpkin — on the seat of a Roman latrine to demonstrate how a Roman might have wiped his bottom. In a world where TV presenters tend to be either "craggy men," as Beard calls them, or smoothly coiffed women with perfect teeth, she is the anti-coif.

The 58-year-old Beard inadvertently became a mascot for older women on television when she appeared in a BBC series without first dyeing her hair.

"It's not like I'm a Stalinist about gray hair," she tells me, sitting in the corner of the coffee shop in her hotel lobby. "In fact, I'd quite like to go pink. But I don't like women feeling like they're *forced* to dye their hair. It raises the broader question: how can women age without falling into the old crone trap? I mean, we're back with the bloody Greeks and Romans."

A. A. Gill, the television critic for *The Sunday Times* and one of Beard's most vicious detractors, has suggested that Beard belongs on *The Undateables*, a reality TV show about people with serious disabilities or disfigurements trying to go on dates. She says that when she first heard about Gill's comments: "For a moment, you feel like someone's hit you. But then you think, this is *silly*. And most of the British public thought it was outrageous. Most women over 50 know what women over 50 look like. And they look like me. They can pretend like they don't, but really they look like me."

She adds, "I'm a classicist, not an autocue girl."

She is, in fact, a very prominent classicist, a professor at the University of Cambridge, the classics editor for *The Times Literary Supplement*, and the author of 12 books on the ancient world.

Her latest, *Confronting the Classics,* is a sprawling collection of essays on everything from Asterix the Gaul to Hannibal. Her approach is decidedly unromantic — she hates it when people get "gooey" about the glories of Rome.

"You do the ancient world much greater service if you keep arguing with them," she says, gesticulating without bothering to put down her latte, which dipped dangerously. "In all sorts of ways they were wrong. But the fact that they were wrong is not as important as the fact that they provided us with a way of thinking. We don't want to go back to the ancient world. Women do not want to go back the ancient world. Jews do not want to go back to the ancient world. Christians do not want to go back to the ancient world. Absolutely *ghastly*." (At this I edge away from the table, fearing burns).

In the book, she writes that the way we read the subject "says as much about us as it does about them." I asked her what she meant. "We raid them," she says, simply. "We have to ventriloquize the ancient world." For example, scholarship on women in the ancient world has grown in the last few decades, Beard says, as a "result of the feminist movements of the '70s and '80s. When I was an undergraduate, people didn't really talk about women in antiquity," she says. But "now, when we talk about Euripides, we talk about his female characters."

If the study of classics, then, can be a mirror of contemporary concerns, it also means scholars are never done. "It's very interesting to look back at classics a hundred years ago. One of the things I've done is look back at Gilbert Murray's translations of Euripides, which were huge popular success at the time. It seemed to engage with all sorts of political issues of the time. And you look at them now, and they're unreadable. People sometimes say that everything's been translated, so why do you need to learn the languages? Well, no, it hasn't — if you want to read the works of Galen, well, *Sorry, sunshine*!"

She says this last wagging her finger at me, as if I had just suggested we pop down to the bookstore for a copy of the collected works of Galen. "You're out of luck," she adds. "You're not going to find a nice English version." (There are, in fact, a few translations of Galen available, but they're not particularly readable).

We also read texts differently in different eras. "It isn't just about putting things into some version of English or French or German or whatever. It's about interpreting the text. It's making this ancient text speak to us in ways we can understand. So translations from a hundred years ago don't hack it for us."

Not to mention that some translations can be plain wrong. As an example, she points to some of the myths surrounding the Roman emperor Caligula, who is famous for sadistic sexual practices. She explains that one frequently mistranslated passage in the work of the historian Suetonius has been used to create an image of garish excess. "The passage is glossed as, 'Caligula had banquets with his wife underneath him and his wife on top,' as if they were in a kind of threesome sandwich. And you look at the Latin, it talks about *intra* and *sufra*, above and underneath, but the words are used as the technical terms for where you sit at a Roman banquet. So someone's on the left and on the right. So there's this whole really lurid version. But *look*, darling, the Latin does not say that. It just doesn't."

Lately, Beard has been doing less work on the Romans than she'd like. Instead, she's been dealing with a relentless stream of anonymous threats, which make crude insults from newspaper columnists seem mild.

Last winter, Beard appeared on the political debate show *Question Time* and argued that the UK can benefit from fewer limits on immigration. Almost immediately, she was inundated with misogynist mail. The website *Don't Start Me Off* named her "Twat of the Week." One person posted a picture of her face superimposed on a vagina. Others speculated about her oral and genital hygiene, or even threatened to rape her. Shocked at the fierceness of the abuse, she decided to reprint some of it on her blog at *The Times Literary Supplement*, "A Don's Life." She wrote in the post, "It would be quite enough to put many women off appearing in public [or] contributing to political debate."

She tells me that "in the UK, you can't actually repeat what they've said. You go on the radio and you have to say, 'He criticized my appearance!' You can't say, 'Actually, what he said is, "You foul cunt, I think your vagina smells of cabbage and I want to roger you with a spatula."' But you just can't *say* that on the BBC. So I just put it up on my blog."

As a result of her post, the website *Don't Start Me Off* was shut down, and the man who owned it apologized to Beard.

"And that got a lot of publicity. Because many people saw it who didn't quite understand what it is when we talk about misogynist abuse. People don't quite realize what it is. So that was a kind of victory." But the victory was short-lived. Feminists in the United Kingdom began a campaign to put a picture of Jane Austen on the pound note. Beard said she supported the campaign, but "wasn't much involved with it." But when the women running it began to get death threats and rape threats, Beard appeared on the radio to talk about dealing with internet abuse.

"And so I said that one of the things to do with threats is retweet them, and show them to the world. And so I was sitting in the radio studio, and there was this guy on Twitter who sent a tweet saying, 'I bet your vagina is really disgusting, you old hag. I bet you won't retweet this!' So, naturally I retweeted it, and within a few minutes, someone said, 'I can tell you where his mother lives.' So I said, let's give him a few hours to apologize. If not, we'll use the mother route. So of course he immediately apologized, and for a while it became a good news story. You know, everybody was saying, 'What do you do with trolls? Tell their mums!' But then I started getting death threats."

"Were you scared?" I ask.

"I think its disingenuous to say you're not scared. You get a note saying 'I'm outside your house,' and for 30 seconds you think, *My god*. After that, was I scared? Not really. I've been around long enough to know that most people, if they want to kill you, they don't send you a tweet first."

Mary Beard's toughness has been built up by decades of dealing with bad press. In the week following 9/11 she infamously wrote in the *London Review of Books* that the United States "had it coming," which provoked an enormous amount of anger on both sides of the Atlantic. It also seems curiously at odds with the way, in her BBC documentary about Pompeii, for example, Mary Beard speaks of the dead — who have been buried in ash for 2,000 years — with genuine sorrow.

I asked her whether she feels the same way about the attacks now, with perhaps, a little more edge than I intended — we are both palpably aware of the mass shooting that had taken place in DC the day before our interview, not far from her hotel.

"I'm glad you asked about that," she says. "Most interviewers are too polite."

She is careful not to apologize, seeming — for the first time — a little uncomfortable:

"I feel that what I was trying to say then, I would still want to say now. I never, ever said that those people deserved to die. That would be monstrous. They were innocent victims. What I was trying to say, and perhaps I wouldn't say it that way now, was that we're mad if we think that Western foreign policy isn't implicated somehow in world terrorism." She pauses cautiously. "No, no, I wouldn't say that. I would say that it is a fair point to make that there is an interrelationship between Western policy — and that's not just the United States — and world terrorism."

"So perhaps you would say it differently?"

"When I wrote that in the couple of days after 9/11, nobody knew how to talk about it. Nobody had a rhetoric. Within two or three weeks, people had actually worked out a way to talk about this that allowed you to disagree. At that moment, we hadn't."

She's sitting still now, hands folded safely on the table.

"If you're a politician, you lose your job if you say the things I've said. It's so easy to just go black and white. But normally the answer is, 'It is more complicated than that.' To say that it's not complicated does not mean that it was a good thing to drive two planes into the Twin Towers. It was a terrible crime. But part of the job of the academic is to be the gadfly. And sometimes that rebounds, and that's a part of it." ⁄⁄

TWO QUESTIONS FOR JUAN FELIPE HERRERA

DANIEL OLIVAS

DANIEL OLIVAS TALKS TO CALIFORNIA'S POET LAUREATE ABOUT TOMÁS RIVERA, BORN IN TEXAS TO MIGRANT FARMWORKERS, WHO BECAME A SIGNIFICANT AUTHOR AND SCHOLAR AND THEN THE FIRST MEXICAN AMERICAN TO SERVE AS THE CHANCELLOR OF A UNIVERSITY OF CALIFORNIA CAMPUS.

DANIEL OLIVAS: It's been almost 30 years since the death of Tomás Rivera, the great Chicano author, poet, and educator whose 1971 novella . . . *y no se lo tragó la tierra* (. . . *and the Earth Did Not Devour Him*) remains required reading in many high schools and colleges. How would you describe his legacy and influence on literature, in general, and on you as a writer, in particular?

JUAN FELIPE HERRERA: Tomás Rivera's legacy is part of all our legacy. That is, in the late 1960s, we were all together; you could almost say we were writing the same thing, or riding in the same wave — different currents perhaps, yet more intimately related as writers, more conscious of our intentions, visions, and even language, idioms, characters, and styles. Tomás stood out because of his intensity, his laser-like focus, and, most of all, his fearlessness in writing about death and suffering. This is where his power breaks free. He was concerned with many "truths" — the truth of the 1940s for farmworkers and the truth of brutality and brilliance in a people's experience. This is where he was different. We generally focused, as writers of a younger generation, on the former, on the brutality. We did not know how to look for that torch of illuminations in a people under the whip. The question of being Mexicano or Chicano or both or neither — somehow, Tomás figured this out (if this is possible) early on. The two are distinct for Tomás: they can be learned, studied, but not necessarily merged by the osmosis of cultural reclamation and symbolic reappropriation — something we craved for in the early years and to some extent continue to do so to this day.

DANIEL OLIVAS: One wonders if Rivera would have trouble getting . . . *y no se lo tragó la tierra* published today. How would you compare publishing in the early days of the Chicano movement with the current publishing environment?

JUAN FELIPE HERRERA: I don't think Rivera would have any difficulty publishing his major work today, as a matter of fact — we finally, I hope, caught up with some of his experiments in form. He would get published in a flat second — his time-space play and his oscillating narrative structure would be recognized as a delicacy.

CLARISSA TOSSIN, "UNMAPPING THE WORLD," 2011, INK ON TRACING PAPER, 29" x 19"

Publishing in the early days was done in garages, as in Alurista's house in San Diego where we would paste up *La Verdad*, a community newspaper, or the centros culturales where we would gather literary "assignments" or as part of talleres, workshops, or in the printing presses of friends associated with our cause, as in the early texts of the *Pocho-Che*, a mesmerizing large-format tabloid put together in the Mission District of San Francisco. The orientation toward publishing was also different. As a matter of fact, we rarely used the word "publishing," or the phrase, "I can't wait to get published." We did it all ourselves, not for "ourselves," but, for others-like-ourselves. "Literary conferences" were more community news, workshop upgrades, and bi-national and international gatherings of artist-friends, if I can put it that way. We were corridistas, singing people traveling, mobilizing in the way poets and writers mobilize and converse and trade stories, ideas, and happenings. A family of 100 poets, 50 teatros, and a handful of novelists in between. Not to mention the mime artists, singing trios and quartets, and an electric guitar and jazz ensemble here and there. The entry and roles of the Danzantes de la Conquista ("Aztec dancers") is another story. So you see, the notion of publishing is too narrow and even anti-cultural in the multi-community orb of what was going on with the Chicana, Chicano, and Americas writers of the mid-1960s through the mid-1970s. Today, well, it's a whole different enchilada. Or, shall we say, a whole different "wrap." //

VOYAGES AROUND THE ROOM

GEOFF NICHOLSON

BERND STIEGLER, *Traveling in Place: A History of Armchair Travel*
TRANSLATED BY PETER FILKINS

XAVIER DE MAISTRE, *Voyage Around My Room*
TRANSLATED BY RICHARD HOWARD AND STEPHEN SARTARELLI

PAUL THEROUX, *The Tao of Travel*

THOMAS PYNCHON, *Bleeding Edge*

There's a story in my family that, when my mother was a girl, she was such a fan of the written word that, as she walked to and from school every day, she always read a book: a habit that ended, perhaps inevitably, when she walked distractedly into a lamppost. I'm not sure what books my mother read in those days, but I like to think she favored rip-roaring adventure stories that took her on wild fictional excursions. Her collision perhaps demonstrated that it's impossible to go on an imaginary journey, while also going on a real one: and perhaps this incident shows that the two are simply incompatible.

———

I've been wondering about the extent to which all literature is essentially travel literature. Don't all books take you out of yourself, take you on a journey, and allow you to visit somewhere you'd never otherwise have gone, possibly somewhere you'd never actually want to be? I've also, of course, been wondering about the extent to which books that are, in the ordinary sense, travel books construct places in much the same way that fiction does. Are de Tocqueville's America or Sir Richard Francis Burton's Mecca any less "constructed" than Kafka's Amerika or James Hilton's Shangri-La?

———

There used to be a gym on the second floor of a building on Sunset Boulevard, with a row of treadmills lined up in front of the windows, overlooking the street. I regularly walked along the sidewalk there, and looked up at the static walkers who were looking down at me, and I suspect we both regarded each other with equal contempt. They, I imagined, thought I was some loser, so pathetic he actually had to walk in order to get places. I, meanwhile, thought they were ludicrous shut-ins: it would do them the power of good to get out and about. I'm not sure that I ever saw any of them reading as they walked, but no doubt some did.

Perhaps I was being too hard on them. There's currently a fad here and there (espoused by Susan Orlean among others) for the "walking workstation," basically a high desk with a treadmill in front of it. Users, says Orlean in a recent *New Yorker* article, "walk at one or two miles per hour, which is slow enough so that it doesn't interfere with typing or talking or reading." She doesn't say whether or not the method "interferes" with thinking or writing, but I have an intuition that it might. I reckon it would make your walking pretty unenjoyable, too. I wonder how Xavier de Maistre would have felt about the walking workstation. De Maistre was the author of *Voyage autour de ma chambre* (1794, with a slightly revised later edition), a title generally translated as *Voyage Around My Room*. After being involved in a duel, he found himself under house arrest in Turin for 42 days, and wrote a journal describing his own room as if he were a traveler exploring an exotic land.

The book consists of 42 short chapters that use various things in the room as inspiration for miniature essays concerning such things as painting, the division between body and soul, and the author's love affairs. The tone is ironic and satirical, with explicit references to Laurence Sterne and Samuel Richardson, but it's not exactly comical. The effect of reading it is a bit like watching one of those jugglers who perform with a single ball: you're pretty sure he's not going to drop it, but you do wonder how he's going to find enough ways of keeping it in the air. It doesn't hurt that de Maistre's book is scarcely 80 pages long.

A long journey across a very short distance has always struck me as a fantastic idea for a book, fiction or non fiction, but it nonfiction. But I was also aware that it had already been done, and that it was an act you couldn't, or shouldn't, try to follow. I was, of course, aware that echoes of de Maistre ring through Huysmans's *À rebours*, Perec's *Life A User's Manual*, and various works by Beckett and Borges (the latter mentions de Maistre by name in his story "The Aleph"). But all those guys have the special dispensations that come with genius. Writing a novel, as Tibor Fischer did in 2003, with the title *Voyage to the End of the Room* seemed to be just asking for trouble, and in the reviews he got it: "a turning point in Fischer's career, the place at which we can no longer offer excuses for his decline," said the *Chicago Tribune*. (It's funny because they're not saying it about me.)

Well, it seems I didn't know the half of it. Thanks to a new book by Bernd Stiegler titled *Traveling in Place: A History of Armchair Travel* (written in 42 short chapters), I learn that all kinds of people have been rash enough to try to out-Maistre de Maistre. Stiegler refers to a whole library of improbable, obscure, and utterly intriguing texts, including such titles as *Voyage dans mes poches* (*Voyage through my pockets*), *Voyage autour de mon cave* (*Voyage around my cellar*), *Voyage dans un tiroir* (*Voyage in a drawer*), and indeed *Voyage autour de ma bibliothèque* (*Voyage around my library*). And that's just the French ones. *Traveling in Place* also discusses Sophie von La Roche's *Mein Schreibetisch* (literally *My Writing Desk*), 1799, two volumes, 850 pages; and Peter Handke's "Die Reise nach La Défense," which describes a visit to La Défense, that notorious Parisian "non-place" where, as Stiegler puts it, "introspection is also presented as a kind of negative epiphany, since it in fact consists of the radical strangeness of the seen, which then correlates to one's own sense of self-alienation."

You won't be surprised to learn that there are many references to Walter Benjamin in Stiegler's book. It was first published in German in 2010 as *Reisender Stillstand: Eine kleine Geschichte des Reisens im und um das Zimmer herum.* That subtitle, which translates as "a short history of travel in and around the room" strikes me as a rather different proposition from the English translation "armchair travel," which for me invokes the image of some old codger sitting by the fire rereading Wilfred Thesiger. The book itself uses the terms "room travel" and "room journey," and I can't help thinking that it must all have sounded snappier term in the original German (*Zimmer-Reisen* presumably), but it's easy enough to see the translator's problem. The term "traveling without traveling" is also used, and that's something every reader knows a good deal about.

Stiegler's remit is encouragingly broad; he refers to the ways in which photography has made armchair travelers of us all, and tells us that, "In Heidelberg, it is a long-established practice to relieve the travel-weary Japanese from having to climb up to the castle: the bus driver simply collects all their cameras in order to take the same pictures from the same perspective with each one while the tourists go shopping or take a break." He covers the movies too, from Dziga Vertov's *Man with a Movie Camera* (in a chapter titled "A Cinematic Baedeker"), to *The Matrix* and *Total Recall.* I was delighted to find a chapter on the movie *Fantastic Voyage* in which a submarine and its crew (including Raquel Welch) are super-miniaturized so they can travel through the bloodstream of an American Cold War scientist, in order to remove a clot. Stiegler writes of "boiling oceans of pink bubbles, excreting walls of guck, jellyfish-like creatures that drift through tunnels that have a cell-like consistency." I wonder if that "guck" is a typo for "gunk," but I like it either way.

Elsewhere, Stiegler deals with those who use trailers or caravans to take their homes with them as they travel: "the most Philistine forms of transport," he says, a bit harshly. But he has to make an exception for Raymond Roussel, author of *Locus Solus,* who created the "Roulette" or Villa Nomade, a motorized vehicle that looks much like a French country cottage on wheels, with a separate servant's quarter for the chauffeur. Roussel used it for a trip to Rome, where he showed it off both to Pope Pius XI and Mussolini. He also tolerates Julio Cortázar and Carol Dunlop's *Autonauts of the Cosmoroute*, published in 2007, in which the authors undertake a month-long journey from Paris to Marseille (less than 500 miles), the whole time spent within their VW bus, on the road, or in rest stops, where they eat, write, and on occasion read tarot cards: "When I turned over the three cards and saw the Chariot of Hermes, I knew. All that comes from this subtle god has always guided me in life […] Now I know we are going to reach our goal."

⁓

The god of the monotheists, I think we can safely say, is not a traveler. When you're omniscient, a visit to a new place is not going to provide any surprises. When you're omnipresent you are, in any case, already there. Adam and Eve in the Garden of Eden could surely have had no concept of what a journey was, though they must have got the hang of it pretty soon after they were expelled.

Stiegler doesn't offer an opinion as to when the tradition of "traveling without traveling" started, but he does mention the Sacri Monti "topographical simulations of religious sites" built in Piedmont and Lombardy from the 15th century onward. These were, and are, a kind of early religious theme park consisting of chapels, or dioramas, containing scenes from the life of Christ, complete with statues of the characters involved, some life-size. Visitors can see the Nativity, the Last Supper, the Via Dolorosa, Calvary, all in an afternoon, and without the inconvenience of going to the Holy Land.

Some would no doubt object that a certain amount of inconvenience is an essential part of any serious journey, spiritual or otherwise; though, I suppose equally, many a Zen sage would say that the journey is the destination, and that heaven lies within, so why the hell would you want to go schlepping across the globe looking for it?

Or perhaps a few years in a hut in the mountains may be all you need. Take the case of Kamo-no-Chōmei, a 12th-century Japanese public servant who, having been passed over for the post of warden of the Kamo shine in Kyoto, withdrew from public life and went into the mountains to become a recluse, and in due course to write a book titled *Hōjōki,* generally translated as *The Ten-Foot-Square Hut.* He lived alone (actually in two different huts) in tranquility for 10 years, while the people of Kyoto experienced various disasters, including earthquakes, fire, and famine.

I couldn't help thinking of those Japanese Hikikomori boys: not mountain dwellers of course, but adolescents who never leave the bedroom in their parents' home, staying put, having their meals left at the door, seeing nobody, but doing a lot of surfing the net and playing video games. If you wanted to make a case that this was in fact just another form of traveling in place, a kind of cyberflaneurism, then you'd get no argument from me. I admit that I only became aware of Kamo-no-Chōmei because he's mentioned in Paul Theroux's slyly subversive personal anthology *The Tao of Travel.* It contains a very short section titled "Staying Home," an alien concept as far as Theroux is concerned, and one that he describes as "suspended animation, if not living death." He includes de Maistre, of course, but also Henry Fielding, whose *Voyage to Lisbon* is concerned, for the first few hundred pages, with delay and diversion. Fielding did get to Lisbon in the end, but died two months after his arrival. Emily Dickinson is also included in Theroux's selection, for her letter to her friend Elizabeth Holland in which she declared that "[t]o shut our eyes is to Travel"; a reasonable compromise, since Dickinson had been housebound for about a decade when she wrote that, and still had another 15 years to live.

Elsewhere in his anthology Theroux suggests that, somewhere along the line, pretty much every travel writer *makes things up*: they only got halfway up the mountain, or they took a bus for part of their great walking expedition, or they said they were alone but really they had a guide and a boyfriend along with them. He doesn't identify any travel book as completely invented from beginning to end, but there must to be some, surely. And certainly the question of whether Marco Polo ever really went to China remains as unsettled as ever. We do know, however, that the account of his travels was written when he was in no position to do any traveling whatsoever, while he was confined to a prison cell in Genoa, where he dictated it to a fellow prisoner, a writer named Rustichello of Pisa. Some readers will be more offended than others by the inventions of travel writers. Personally, I've always had problems with Bruce Chatwin. In the early '90s, I had a writing commission to visit the Australian desert, including Alice Springs. Foolishly, as it turned out, I read Chatwin's *The Songlines* before I went. I thought it was great, and it created a very clear mental image of the place for me, but when I got there that image bore absolutely no relation to what I saw and experienced on the ground. These days I'm prepared to take most of the blame, to admit that I probably imagined too intensely and rigidly, but really, Alice Springs (per *The Songlines*) was not "a grid of scorching streets where men in long white socks were forever getting in and out of Land Cruisers." It just wasn't.

I've never quite trusted Chatwin since then, and Theroux does suggest that he had moments of feverish invention, though sometimes it seems he actually underplayed his adventures. Theroux quotes a line from Chatwin's *In Patagonia*: "I left the Rio Negro and went on south, to Port Madryn," thereby glossing over a massively long trek on foot; whereas in a letter home to his wife he wrote, "dying of tiredness. Have just walked 150 odd miles."

⁓

For the reader of fiction, the possible objections to inventions of place are quite different. Yes, London, Los Angeles, New York are real cities that you can visit, but all those literary walking tours of, say, Dickens's London, or Chandler's Los Angeles, or Salinger's New York, somehow miss the point. These places can only be visited by way of literature. However *literally* a novelist describes a place, it will always be fictional.

There are moving targets here, of course: our experience both of text and place changes all time. When I first read *Gravity's Rainbow*, I would have said that the London that Thomas Pynchon depicted in the first section of that book was somehow "unconvincing," but now I'm not sure what I even meant by that. Naturally, I wasn't in wartime London any more than Pynchon was. My and his knowledge came inevitably from secondary sources; movies, images, and texts. As I reread his novel today, however, Pynchon's London strikes me as perfectly persuasive, and above all as one more version in a universe of infinitely variable and divergent Londons. Topographic accuracy counts for something, but in the end not for very much. We don't want our London authors to place Southwark north of the Thames when it's in fact in the south, but if they choose to locate within the city a giant, wandering adenoid, then that's just fine.

I believe (to the extent that one rationally believes things about Pynchon) that he did live in London in the late 1970s, well after he'd written *Gravity's Rainbow*. We have it on pretty good authority that he's lived in New York for several decades, which I think means we tend to hold his version of New York, the one created in his latest novel *Bleeding Edge*, to a higher standard. I think this is true of all writers associated with a specific city. We expect some insider information, something that the tourist, or even the determined explorer, wouldn't know about. We don't want simply to be told that London is a set of "villages," that Los Angeles sprawls, that New York has concrete canyons. We want something true but unexpected. Raymond Chandler's greatness is apparent in his descriptions of mean streets and Santa Ana winds, but his description of L.A. in the rain in the beginning of *The Big Sleep* is the mark of his absolute *genius*.

I was living in New York in 2001, the year that *Bleeding Edge* is set, though I suspect I wasn't hanging out in any of the same locales as Tommy P, and I don't know how much of a flaneur Pynchon is, but one way or another the inhabitants of New York do inevitably get out and about, spend a certain amount of time pounding the streets, becoming flaneurs by default. I was glad that *Bleeding Edge* avoids the more obvious or literal forms of historical "accuracy." Was there really a bar that sold Zima on tap? Was there really a Chinese restaurant that served The Gang of Four Vegetarian Combo and Szechuan Muesli? I stand to be corrected, but I don't think so. In any case, this in no way impinges on the authenticity of Pynchon's fictional city. As a reader, I believe it all.

Equally, I don't think it matters whether or not there really were teachers who

> announced that there shall be no more fictional reading assignments [...] Somebody needs this nation of starers believing they're all wised up at last, hardened and hip to the human conditions, freed from the fictions that led them so astray, as if paying attention to made up lives was some form of *evil drug abuse*.

Maybe Pynchon just made it up, but I find it completely plausible, perfectly authentic.

Still, if the teachers and pupils of New York really had abandoned fictional reading assignments, I suppose it would have been possible (though highly unlikely) that they could have read de Maistre's *Voyage Around My Room* with a clear conscience. The guy really did voyage around his room! In the last chapter, as he's about to be freed, he writes,

> They may have forbidden me to travel through a city, one place, but they left me the entire universe: infinity and eternity are at my command. So today is the day of my freedom, or rather the day I shall put my shackles back on.

Still, I'm sure it did him the power of good to get out and about. ⁄⁄

AMANDA ROSS-HO, ***DROPCLOTH QUILT #2***, 2011, DROPCLOTH, COTTON, THREAD
SEWN BY GINA ROSS, 71.5" X 52.5"
COURTESY OF THE ARTIST AND MITCHELL-INNES AND NASH, NEW YORK
PHOTO CREDIT: CHRISTOPHER BURKE STUDIO

SIGNS OF LIFE

FRANCESCA LIA BLOCK

My brother kept my mother's ashes in a black plastic box in his closet. Three years passed and we were unable to do anything with them.

Finally I called a burial-at-sea place in Santa Barbara, where my mother had briefly lived in a Spanish apartment building off State Street, in a studio filled with dried pink roses, small, faded oriental rugs, and my father's paintings of my mother playing her lute. My brother drove my children and me along the blue coast, into the town, and through to the harbor. I said to my kids, "Look for signs of magic from Grandma." I didn't tell them to look for signs of life.

The day was temperate and glistening. The crusty captain had rotten teeth, and we paid him to take us into the water on a boat that had my daughter's name. There were sea lions sleeping in a heap on a post, lolling and baying. They are some of my favorite animals — fat mermaids that make the hairs on the back of my neck stand up with wonder. The captain said they aren't called sea lions for nothing; they will attack and bite. My daughter took a picture of my brother and me. I look fair-haired and peaceful like my mother in it; to look like her was the only thing I ever really wanted when I was a child. Hundreds of feet of kelp drifted through the water, like mermaid tails, when we got out far enough to scatter the ashes. My brother read a poem about what happens when your mother dies. Something about needles in your throat. I spoke to my family and told them why I love them. My mother's voice came through me with great ease, and her tears mingled with mine. "Jasmine, I love you for your strength. I am so proud of the woman you are becoming. Sam, for your sweetness. You are the kindest person I know. When you were a baby you cried if an animal was hurt in a movie. You are still always this kind. Gregg, for your generosity. You took care of me when no one else did, when I needed you most." We scattered my mother's ashes into the sea. The bits of bone among the soft gray powder were disturbing. My children did not seem afraid of them. Maybe they didn't realize what they were. My daughter, in the glinting sunlight, looked, with her pale eyebrows, deep-set eyes, heart-shaped face, and long hair, exactly like my mother. Some bad rock band playing on shore was our soundtrack. We scattered white roses tinged with pink at the edges as if they had been dipped in paint. We cried, inhaling ash that dusted our hands and clothes, and my daughter got seasick. We went back to shore, washed our hands, and ate at a courtyard restaurant. I ate fish because there was nothing vegan on the menu that had protein. I felt a weird animal buzz. My children had waffles with whipped cream and giant ice cream waffle cones for dessert.

We drove home through bad traffic. No one argued. I said to my daughter, "Maybe Grandma will provide us with the perfect movie to watch tonight." She said, "I think she's out of magical things." The movie was a funny love story about a mother and daughter who fight but end up happily ever after. //

THE SARTRE SCENARIO

MICHAEL WOOD

JEAN-PAUL SARTRE, *The Freud Scenario*
TRANSLATED BY QUINTIN HOARE

JEAN-PAUL SARTRE, *We Have Only This Life To Live*

In 1959, at the invitation of John Huston, Jean-Paul Sartre wrote a long screenplay about the life of Sigmund Freud. Huston asked for some cuts and Sartre obliged, but also added a lot more than he had taken out. These difficulties might have been overcome if Huston had not invited Sartre to his house in Ireland. Both men left petulant records of the encounter. Sartre said the atmosphere was that of "a vast cemetery," and Huston claimed it was impossible to hold a conversation with his guest: "there was no interrupting him." Quite a few scenes in the finished film (*Freud: The Secret Passion*, 1962, with Montgomery Clift and Susannah York) follow Sartre's screenplay closely, but he didn't want his name on it; the credit went instead to Charles Kaufman and Wolfgang Reinhardt.

Sartre's ambivalence toward Freud was longstanding. Back in 1943 he had been scornful of "the crude, questionable methods of Freud, Adler, or Jung": "There are other schools of psychoanalysis," he said, "il y a d'autres psychoanalyses." By 1969 he was describing himself as a "critical fellow-traveller" of psychoanalysis as it had become constituted in France and elsewhere, but not everyone was convinced he had changed his position all that much. The problem was that he was introducing, in his review *Les Temps modernes*, a "Psychoanalytic Dialogue" in which a patient berates his analyst as an appalling, unmitigated tyrant. Sartre admired the patient's bid for freedom, and his two commentators, J.B. Pontalis, later the editor of Sartre's *Freud* script, and Bernard Pingaud, a writer who describes himself as "neither analyst nor analysand," thought Sartre had totally missed the point of Freud's work and everything that came after it (all this is in *Situations, IX*, Gallimard, 1972). This ambivalence, if that is what it is, certainly shapes the script as we have it in its published version, which first appeared in French in 1984, in English in 1985, and is now reprinted.

Both Sartre and Huston were interested in Freud's early career. Their sources were the first volume of Ernest Jones's biography and the exchange of letters between Freud and Wilhelm Fliess. The screenplay has three parts that are something like musical movements. They represent the discovery that hatred of or excessive identification with the father is at the heart of many neuroses, including Freud's own; the recognition of the functioning of transference; and the liberating perception that if all are guilty, no one is guilty — a sort of refutation of *The*

Brothers Karamazov. Celebrated patients come and go: Anna O., here called Cäcilie; Dora. Freud quarrels with and breaks with his mentor Theodor Meynert, who finally confesses to his own hysteria. Freud works with Josef Breuer, and understands a great deal about the sexual self that Breuer can only deny. This denial becomes the Sartrean sin of bad faith, although only the omniscient writer of the script knows about it: "His bad faith is far too profound to be detected." Not detectable but detected all the same, and identifiable as bad faith. This is either a radically new take on the unconscious — it's not just structured like a language, as Freud's successor Jacques Lacan says: it speaks our language impeccably, even allows for moral judgments — or a failure to understand what the unconscious is. Wouldn't repression in its way always be an instance of good faith?

There are Sartrean paradoxes and epigrams everywhere in *The Freud Scenario*: "I wasn't young during my youth"; "No, Madam, you don't see but you're not blind"; "Everything is important"; "Everything is always faked"; "Oedipus is everybody." There is much talk — strangely, for a story about a Jewish atheist — of hell and the devil. And at moments the glare of hindsight becomes rather strong: "Do you know what I dream of writing? A psychopathology of everyday life." It all seems a little comic at this stage; Mel Brooks and Woody Allen have passed this way too often.

Still, there is real drama in Sartre's understanding of how psychoanalytic transference works. The patients "transfer on to the doctor a forbidden or impossible feeling they were entertaining for someone else." But then the doctor may have an untransferred feeling for an attractive patient, and the very Sartrean thought that "we know ourselves through others, we know others through ourselves" becomes a nightmare. We see in others the displacements of our own story as they see their displaced story in us. All kinds of horrors are possible here, including Freud's recurring fear that he may desire his own daughter. He doesn't, but he might. How would he know?

Most often the screenplay retreats to what people do know, and the visible counterpart of a too profound bad faith is the practice of compensation and concealment: "The more conscious he is of lying, the more firm and stubborn he appears." And indeed the dominant emotion of the screenplay is a kind of willed rage, as if the havoc of the unconscious could be kept at bay, possibly even canceled by the fury we consciously conjure up and direct. There is much talk throughout of irritation (we see Freud's wife, Martha, "laughing but irritated really" and "torn between [. . .] irritation and [. . .] anxiety"; Freud is "irritated" when he contradicts Dora; Breuer's wife is talkative "above all out of irritation"), and of anger (Freud is "beside himself with rage," turns "white with anger," and finds himself "bristling with rage"; Martha goes "pale with anger"; Meynert drinks his schnapps "angrily"). But the real category of choice is fury: in one scene both Freud and Martha are "furious"; Freud is "in a fury"; Breuer's wife is "beside herself with fury"; Freud is furious with Cäcilie, with Breuer, and gets "furious at his own docility." (This last instance points us back to the curious terrain where Sartre seems both to understand and fail to understand the workings of the unconscious.) There is a good deal of reference, too, to violence: Breuer's wife speaks with "an almost vulgar violence," Cäcilie "with sudden and terrible violence," and Freud himself talks "violently"; his attitude to Martha combines "ardour, jealousy, violence." "He has become," we are told at one point, "a man of violence, ready to violate his patients' consciousness to satisfy his scientific curiosity" — here we meet the analyst-as-tyrant of Sartre's comment on the 1969 "Psychoanalytic Dialogue." In the same vein, Freud speaks "with sovereign authority — but [. . .] with a suppressed violence." It's true these effects are all in the stage directions and descriptions of action; true, too, that Montgomery Clift in Huston's movie looks haunted and sorrowful rather than angry. But the language of Sartre's screenplay really is obsessive, itself crying out for analysis.

What do we make of this? If we are thinking about a film — either the one that was completed or the one that wasn't — we don't have to make anything of it, since it will all have vanished into real or imagined gestures and expressions, will have survived its acting out or not. We can comment on that result, even the virtual one. But if we are thinking about Sartre's work, we need to attend to the text in front of us.

J.B. Pontalis, in his introduction, prolongs his delicate skepticism about what Sartre was doing with *The Freud Scenario*. He suggests that Sartre was interested in Freud because psychoanalysis was "the product of a long activity carried out upon himself — and above all, which counted for much more in Sartre's eyes, *against* himself." This remark is followed by a discreet barb: "Sartre used to take the greatest pleasure in seeing his ideas overthrown, always provided he was the one to draw the consequences." Against himself indeed. Pontalis goes on to say that Sartre's work on the *Freud* screenplay created the intellectual conditions for the writing of his great book on Flaubert, *The Family Idiot* (1971–'72): "I would tend to think that the 'Freud' made the 'Flaubert' possible." This is not quite the same as saying Sartre had got the hang of psychoanalysis, and Pontalis's irony continues to be both gentle and precise:

> The trouble is that to Sartre's blunt, insistent question: "What can we know about a man?" — to that question which is not its own — psychoanalysis can offer only a disappointing reply: not "Nothing," but "What man has always known."

With this reply in mind we can see that the *Freud* screenplay allows two gaps to open up to a degree of impassibility that Sartre himself found it difficult to acknowledge: between what we see and what we know of others; and between what we know of ourselves and who we are. The gaps are not unbridgeable themselves, of course; we cross them all the time. But the separate realms may speak different languages, and therefore be connectable only by translation or indirection. This is precisely the trouble that Sartre's screenplay runs into and reveals. Sartre the Cartesian can't really believe in what is "too profound to be detected" — it'll be detected somehow, its mystery stripped away — and he is too much the existential explorer to lay much store by "what man has always known." The fury in the script expresses what can't be expressed, as well as a kind of annoyance at the survival of so much murky residue. What can we not know about a man? ⁄⁄

Oh Wow

MICHAEL ROBBINS

The only reason you're not going to hell is you're already in it.

The *Fear Factor* contestant says he's in it to win it.

Science, the opiate of the elite, asks too many questions.

I become tired and sick, till I wander off by myself and listen in perfect
    silence to *The Sun Sessions*.

Why is there something rather than something else is a question only
    Southern rock can answer.

The cattle all have brucellosis. Grandma's dead of cancer.

The astronauts of my youth plant the flashing MTV logo on the moon.

I thought of that historic moment on the day Steve Jobs was taken from us too soon.

The artist formerly known as Sting gives backrubs to the war orphans;

Swami Svatmarama distributes copies of the *Hatha Yoga* to boost the orphans'
    endorphins.

Would you care to make a small donation?

The orphans with remaining limbs give the dharma a standing ovation.

Oh wow, a guy came on your face and you wrote about it? That's so daring.

Let me be among the very first to say thanks for sharing.

If you need a writing tutor, I am programmed to oblige.

Lesson one: metaphor, a kind of bridge.

A blackbird can be looked at in a number of ways, including two.

A man and a woman are the loneliest number that you'll ever do.

CELL PHONE DIARIES

DINAH LENNEY

"Echo Park Lake is almost back [. . .] Before it was refilled [. . .]
workers found two guns, one toilet, 20 Frisbees and a pay telephone."
—*Los Angeles Times,* May 11, 2013

I'm seated next to a colleague at a celebratory dinner (a charming youngish man), delighted to have his attention, of course I am, waiting for my salmon fillet with no bigger fish to fry. Whereas my youthful friend, a writer of note, is on assignment facing a deadline (he's told me so), expecting notes from his editor any minute. So I shouldn't be surprised when he pulls his phone out of his pocket. But I am — a little — surprised and the tiniest bit put out, too; mock-insulted, but sort of appalled (*this really can't wait?*), and I snap — half in fun, as if he were my brother, or even my son — "You put that thing away." He, in turn, feigns shame: dutifully shoves the *thing*, slim and gleaming, back into his pocket as if we'd rehearsed. Although we both know he's indulging me — that it's okay for him to have the phone at the table: acceptable not just to sneak a look now and then, but also to actually be in two conversations at once. Some of you are just that good: you can chat each other up as you make the requested changes, and all before pudding is served.

—

A few months ago, we invited a couple (in town for his birthday) for drinks before dinner in Chinatown, where we drove in separate cars — each spouse with the other (since we knew the way, and they didn't). When she and I arrived at the restaurant, they were already seated: my husband was absently arranging his chopsticks, while hers madly scrolled and typed into his phone. Who could blame him, it being his birthday? Who could fault this affable guy for reading and texting straight through the meal — from fried dumplings to fortune cookies — especially since he didn't miss a beat, fluently conversed, deftly fielded questions about health care, the Middle East, the Supreme Court, movies, books, art, even as he chatted up relatives and friends across the country. In this case, I wasn't about to play his big sister — we're not that chummy, for one thing, plus he has kids of his own — but remember when messages were messages? Remember when we came home at the end of the day and answered them?

—

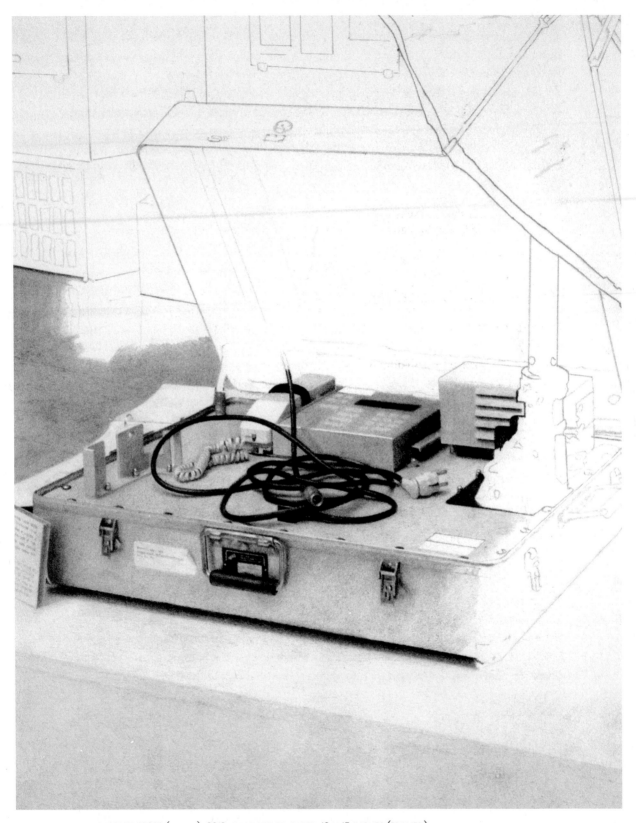

MATT SIEGLE, ***PHONE 1991(?)/2009*** (DETAIL), 2012, GRAPHITE ON PAPER, 19 X 15 INCHES (FRAMED)

Why, I ask my husband, do you have to take that call? We're hiking with the dog. The birds are chirping, the squirrels are chittering, when his phone clangs. Which is better than the theme from *Close Encounters*, I guess, but couldn't he have left it home?

He has explained that my values are not only arcane, but also irrelevant. What's more, he wants to know why he can't ever reach me: "Don't you answer your phone?" he accuses. And one evening when he texts and then calls while I'm at an event (and he *knows* where I am), his voicemail actually sounds hurt. He wants me to join the real world, which means, I can only suppose, that I should abandon it for the virtual one.

—«—

How often have I congratulated my juggling self? Watch me set the table, feed the dog, answer the phone, scribble a message — all while stirring the Bolognese with my big wooden spoon — but, I've recently discovered, I'm not all that talented. See, if you're not distracted by that call or text, I am. I'm the woman who takes her eyes from the big screen when a little one lights up three rows down; I hear the buzzing in your bag: what's more, I confess, I cringe, mortified, when the creature from another planet turns out to be in my own. And when we're having a drink at that wine bar on Sunset near Alvarado? It's all I can do not to let my eyes stray to your screen. In which case, I can only assume — does this makes sense, please? — that I'm the one with bad manners.

Except don't you expect me to listen when you're talking on the phone in the bank, at the counter, on the corner, and especially in the adjacent stall? And I know, you don't care what I think: but what about the person on the other end of the line, that's what I'm asking. *So tragic*, you say. And then: *She found him, poor thing ... Oh I know, all those flowers ... His sister sang, don't know how she got through it ... Me too, I hate an open casket* — wait a sec: a metallic hiccup, then another — my god, are you wiping? Have you put the phone down so you can wipe? And what about me: should I flush, or should I wait, or — or what should I do?

—«—

Remember phone booths? Designed so as to remove the caller from the fray? To actually face her away from the crowd? Remember when there was a designated spot, or a row of them, but if you were in the row, you were probably minding your own business, or if you were eavesdropping, it was understood that *you* were the one abusing the privilege?

—«—

I've noticed, have you? Two people conversing in a public place will lean in and lower their voices — moreover, we'll avert our eyes if caught overhearing them. However: a person on a cell phone thinks nothing of shouting into it as if he had his own television show. So it appears, doesn't it, that if we're actually acquainted with our audience — who might, therefore, forgive our bad manners — we'll conduct ourselves with some kind of decorum. Whereas if not (if we feel anonymous), we're not just willing but wired to privately exult or grieve or wax on at extraordinary decibels about the most ordinary things.

So here's what I'm asking: not what's more compelling — the real or the virtual — but if there's even any difference anymore. Do you stand to miss something if you dine with or without your phone in your lap? I guess that depends on who's coming to dinner ...

We're at the Hollywood Bowl for a concert. A noisy clan has the next row down, and the woman in front of me is holding out her phone, snapping photos of herself and her date, not one, not two — 10 flashes, 15, 20, 21, 22 — when I ask her to stop.

"You're blinding me," I say.

"I'm trying to capture a moment," says she.

Next to her, her sister, or friend, or whatever she is, is videotaping — not the stage but one of the jumbo screens (there are three). Beside her, a boy is playing a game on his phone, and on the other side of him (this is novel), a young man is actually *talking* into his, and straight through a show-stopping ballad, too. "I can't believe we got these seats," he shouts. Me neither. From up here in the nosebleeds (would it have been different in promenade two or three?), the singer on the stage flits about like a butterfly, but never mind her — the moment, not quite captured, appears to be happening up here in section R2, flash number 23. We give up. Home we go, before intermission.

Sunday in the park, and just ahead, a woman and a man with a baby in a stroller are stopped in the middle of the path. He's shouting at her back: "We're not on the phone! We're on a walk!"

By the time I pass, she's hung up and is striding ahead while he hops around behind her in a fury. "It was work," she spits over her shoulder. "I don't care," he screams, "I don't give a fuck! I'd like to break that thing in half!"

Back at the airport, we're standing at the sinks, my stall-mate and I; phone balanced between her ear and her shoulder, she's rummaging for something in her makeup bag and taking her time about it, too. Whereas I'm rushing. To give her privacy. In the restroom. At LAX. As I turn to the dryers (the noisy kind — is it all right to activate? Should I wipe on the seat of my pants, and get the hell out?), she leans into the mirror to pick at something between her front teeth. *Oh I know*, she says, yadda yadda, *the most beautiful memorial*, yadda yadda yadda, she was so very moved, she will never, not ever, be the same. ✍

CROWD CONTROL

LEO BRAUDY

Steven Spielberg, despite 29 feature films and numerous awards, and despite being ritually genuflected to by hordes of young filmmakers and wannabes, seems very anxious about the effects his films will have on an audience. So anxious, in fact, that in many of his films he includes an audience *within* the film so that we in the theater, sitting there in the dark, will have a model of how to behave, appreciate, cheer, and perhaps even genuflect to.

Some of the most memorable scenes in Spielberg's first big moneymaker, *The Sugarland Express* (1974), for instance, involve two fugitives and their hostage being trailed by an enormous task force of police cars, news vans, and helicopters, and observed by roadside gawkers as they make their slow-moving way across Texas. In *Close Encounters of the Third Kind* (1977), after a long buildup focusing on the almost entirely solitary quest of Roy Neary (Richard Dreyfuss) to justify his obsession with a certain monolith in Wyoming, the virtually endless last scene — even more endless in the director's cut — expands the dramatis personae to include a whole flotilla of technicians, scientists, and government officials to witness the landing of the saucer. In each successive Indiana Jones sequel, the crowds increase. Can Indy just shoot his scimitar-wielding attacker in *Raiders of the Lost Ark* (1981)? No, he has to do it in front of a souk's worth of onlookers. Can Indy rescue Short Round from the flaming pit and let just the audience in the theater appreciate his derring-do? No, he needs all the Temple of Doom acolytes to ooh and aah repeatedly as he twists and turns above the inferno. Then, too, is it really necessary that the entire neighborhood turn out to bear witness to the government medical facility set up in Elliott's house?

This tendency to underline dramatic action by the presence of a group (or a mass) of onscreen viewers may explain why *Lincoln* (2012) didn't end with the president's solitary walk down the corridor away from us, but then had to include Ford's Theater and the death scene, with the surrounding mourners weighing in with their familiar lines? Everyone who attended grammar school knew what was going to happen when Lincoln walked away, but for some reason Spielberg couldn't let us appreciate the dramatic irony by ourselves: he needed the group scene to make sure we got the point.

Not all Spielberg's films are this way. His first real success, *Duel* (1971), is a spare drama with only two main characters, which takes place on remote roads in the midst of unpeopled landscapes. And in *A.I.* (2001) the isolated protagonists never manage to link up with any group at all. I could include *The Terminal* (2004) in this group as well, although its saga of a man unnoticed in one of the most teeming and transient places we ever pass through has ironies enough. Such films, however, are outweighed in Spielberg's career by those in which a somewhat solitary central character does or discovers something unusual, and is witnessed doing so by a crowd. His great populist forebear Frank Capra staged comparable scenes in *Mr. Smith Goes to Washington* and *It's a Wonderful Life*. But they arose much more directly from the plot, while Spielberg's seem nervously lathered on.

Do such scenes function as an allegory of Spielberg's own career, the outsider become insider? Are they instead tenacious vestiges of insecurity about the audience's response to his visions and fantasies? Or is it, like the sonorous John Williams music so often verging on bombast, just another way to ensure that we know we're being entertained? Whatever the reason, Spielberg seems unwilling at times, despite his success, to trust audiences to respond freely, on their own, to his art. ⁄⁄

THE KNOWN WORLD

COLIN DICKEY

The Arctic archipelago of Svalbard is largely desolate, with just a few thousand people spread across its bleak terrain. The main settlement is a town called Longyearbyen; at just over 2,000 residents, it's the world's northernmost town with a population of more than 1,000 people. Once it was a thriving coal settlement; now the decaying wood ruins of past mining operations hover like ghosts, and the town has largely become a tourist hub, home to a cruise ship terminus, hotels, museums (including one devoted entirely to aeronautical attempts to overfly the North Pole in balloons), and, farther into the valley, an art gallery, where I found, on exhibition during my stay there, a collection of old arctic maps. Filling three full rooms, they laid out the sporadic evolution of how we have come to know the Arctic Circle, from medieval maps that presumed fictitious islands and hearsay continents, to early modern projections both more detailed and more honest in their ignorance, their carefully drawn coastlines eventually giving way to indistinct outlines and then to white space, legended "The Frozen Sea," or "Parts Unknown."

To fill these blank spaces, mapmakers added flourishes and elaborate illustrations. In one labeled "A Map of the North-Pole and the Parts Adjoining," trappers and whalers hunt sea creatures somewhere between whales and walruses. In another a bearded cherub points to a name — "Spitzberga" — emblazoned on a shield supported by a pair of whiskered fish. Above the legend of a map of Novaya Zemlya, a hunter pulled on a sledge by a leaping reindeer takes aim with his bow at a rearing bear, while below him men carry dead walruses like sacks of potatoes and a woman milks horned goats. Others still have darker images: not just idyllic scenes of hunter and prey, but strange lion-headed fish, scaly whales with dual blowholes, and, on one, a walrus with a human face and hair: a "seamorce," described as "bigg as an oxe."

Among those who took aim at these fantastical beasts was Sir Thomas Browne, who sought to dispel myths and long-held errors in his encyclopedic *Pseudodoxia Epidemica* (1646–1672). Writing, for example, of Sea-horses (meaning not the small fish in the genus *Hippocampus* but the full-sized, aquatic steeds often depicted in atlases), Browne comments that they "are but *grotesco* delineations, which fill up empty spaces in Maps, and meer pictoriall inventions, not any Physicall shapes." The monster, he suggests, is the illustrator's equivalent of the cartographer's "Parts Unknown." A century after Browne, Jonathan Swift made a similar comment in his 1733 lyric "On Poetry: A Rhapsody":

So Geographers in Afric-Maps
With Savage-Pictures fill their Gaps;
And o'er unhabitable downs
Place Elephants for want of Towns.

But I have always been far more intrigued with these strange shapes and figures, with these seeming afterthoughts, than with the rest of the map. For some time I've studied medieval marginalia, the way monks and other copyists would decorate holy scriptures and other literature with bawdy images of nuns breast-feeding monkeys, mer-creatures shooting arrows into men's asses, rabbit funerals in which foxes acted as pallbearers. The images on the maps in Svalbard weren't quite as inscrutable, but they did work to interpret the landscape differently than the maps they adorned, telling a narrative alongside the map's spatial translation of the world.

Such marginalia is for the most part long dead. On a webpage, there may be peripheral images, ads, or other visual interference — but there's not the same sense of empty space that needs filling, no epistemological need to doodle away the white void. A webpage is always exactly as big or as small as it wants to be. A printed page, or a map, on the other hand, sometimes it has extra space, and what artists have chosen to put in that space can mean a great deal, the visual ornamentation framing the information and directing the eye.

⁓

I left Longyearbyen aboard a ship that would take me up the western coast of Svalbard. I was there in the company of 25 other artists, writers, and scientists, as part of a residency called the Arctic Circle. For two weeks we lived on a three-masted sailing ship that took us through fjords and open water in a barely inhabited world. During that time I thought some of Naglfar, the "nail ship" described in the 13th-century *Prose Edda*, a ship from Hell, made from the finger- and toenails of the dead. At the End of the World the Wolf Skoll will swallow the sun and his brother Hati the moon, and the stars shall vanish from the sky. In the midst of a cataclysm, the Naglfar shall be set loose and bring the dead to the land of the living for the great and final battle. As the *Prose Edda* warns, "if a man die with unshorn nails, that man adds much material to the ship Naglfar, which gods and men were fain to have finished late." I also thought of monsters, of how ancient sailors looked at the backs of whales, the remnants of squid, or perhaps a narwhal tusk, and saw in them horrors, terrifying menaces. As we sailed out into open waters, into an endless barrage of punishing waves that sickened half the passengers, I thought of those horrible creatures lurking in the open white of those old maps, a warning to other mariners of what lay out there. Those ancient map images had begun, you could say, to frame my voyage as well. I carried them in my mind for the next few weeks, attempting to superimpose their gridded and mathematical lines and their grotesque monsters onto the slate gray and formless arctic sea before me.

Among the most fascinating examples of these maps, covered with all manner of fantastical creatures, is Olaus Magnus's *Carta Marina*. Born in Sweden in 1490, Olaus, a Catholic priest, was working abroad in Gdańsk when, in 1527, Protestants took over his homeland, resulting in his permanent exile. Olaus eventually settled in Rome, and in time would be made the last archbishop of Uppsala (a largely ceremonial title, since he could not return to Sweden). Working as something of a cultural ambassador from Scandinavia, he wrote in exile, recreating his home in his writing and his great map.

Olaus's map is huge — one of the largest charts in both physical size and the scope it covered. It was lost for centuries, until discovered in 1886 by Oscar Brenner. (A second copy, the only other extant, was found in 1962.) The intervening time did not serve it well; 20th-century scholars have long faulted Olaus's cartographical ignorance, and his placing of the Arctic Circle at 90 degrees, rather than at 66. As one critic wrote in 1949:

> The map is an interesting example of a compiler failing to understand the character of his materials, and falling into an error which was perpetuated by his successors. Important as was Olaus' work as the historian of the north, he scarcely emerges from a critical examination as a cartographer of great competence.

But to look to Olaus for scientific accuracy would miss the point. In 1555 he produced his other great work, *Historia de gentibus septentrionalibus* ("A History of the Northern Peoples," literally the "People Under the Seven Stars," meaning the constellation the Big Dipper). In it he offered the first serious discussion of snowflakes, of which he wrote: "it seems more a matter for amazement than enquiry why and how so many shapes and forms, which elude the skill of any artist you choose to name, are so suddenly stamped upon such soft, tiny objects." Olaus was as much interested in amazement as competence, as much interested in wonder as in accuracy.

Joseph Nigg's coffee-table exploration of Olaus's map, *Sea Monsters: A Voyage Around the World's Most Beguiling Map*, draws our attention away from the traditional function of the map, pulling the monsters out of the borders and into the frame. It is, for Nigg ("one of the world's leading experts on fantastical animals," according to his bio), the geography and cartography that become inessential; the "map" he's interested in is not of land but of beasts. Nigg traces an imaginary voyage through Olaus's heavily populated seas, past a Polypus (a "Creature with many feet, which hath a pipe on his back […] with his Legs as it were by hollow places, dispersed here and there, and by his Toothed Nippers, he fastneth on every living Creature that comes near to him, that wants blood"); a Sea Swine ("it had a Hogs head, and a quarter of a Circle, like the Moon, in the hinder part of its head, four feet like a Dragons, two eyes on both sides of his Loyns, and a third in his belly inkling towards his Navel; behind he had a Forked-Tail, like to other fish commonly"); a Prister (a "kind of Whales, two hundred Cubits long […] very cruel. For to the danger of Sea-men, he will sometimes raise himself beyond the Sail-yards, and casts such floods of Waters above his head, which he had sucked in, that with a Cloud of them, he will often sink the strongest ships, or expose the Mariners to extream danger."); and the terrifying Ziphius ("He hath as ugly a head as an Owl; His mouth is wondrous deep, as a vast pit, whereby he terrifies and drives away those that look into it. His Eyes are horrible, his back Wedge-fashion, or elevated like a sword; his Snout is

JOHNNY HARRIS, *MAPS*, 2013

pointed." "It will swim under ships, and cut them, that the Water may come in, and he may feed on the men when the ship is drown'd."). Each monster is given Olaus's description, an inquiry into Olaus's inspirations, and its subsequent legacy.

The Polypus, for example, is drawn as a 15-foot lobster, but Nigg notes that its description more closely resembles an octopus. This is what makes Olaus's map (and, by extension, Nigg's book) so fascinating: for all its basis in medieval bestiaries, the map is also a serious attempt to catalog the denizens of the deep. Olaus relied on oral legend, folklore, and his own memories, all of which he gathered and reported as faithfully as he could — a Brother Grimm of oceanographic mythology. As Nigg points out, "Regardless of how fantastically the creatures are portrayed on the map, they are meant to represent actual marine animals." And at least some of them do: Olaus's map contains perhaps the first image of a whale nursing her calf; the first depiction of a real oceanographic feature, the Iceland-Faroe Front; and the first mention of a narwhal, albeit under a different name:

> The Unicorn is a Sea-Beast, having in his Fore-head a very great Horn, wherewith he can penetrate and destroy the ships in his way, and drown multitudes of men. But divine goodnesse hath provided for the safety of the Mariners herein; for though he be a very fierce Creature, yet is he very slow, that such as fear his coming may fly from him.

In terms of the narwhal's behavior, Olaus was mostly wrong — it does not attack mariners, nor is it that slow, but while we know more than Olaus did, we don't know that much more — "We know more about the rings of Saturn than we know about the narwhal," Barry Lopez writes in *Arctic Dreams*. We don't even know much about the name we gave it — many claim that the word "narwhal" means "corpse-whale," so named for the animal's pale color, as though of a dead body, but Lopez and others dispute this etymology. What's clear is that, with the male's unicorn tusk growing as long as nine feet in length, it seems to defy all our standard rules of animal physiology. Lopez writes of seeing two narwhals in Lancaster Sound in 1982, a startling place to see animals so rare:

> The day I saw them I knew that no element of the earth's natural history had ever before brought me so far, so suddenly. It was as though something from a bestiary had taken shape, a creature strange as a giraffe. It was as if the testimony of someone I had no reason to doubt, yet could not quite believe, a story too farfetched, had been verified at a glance.

We ourselves saw no narwhals on our voyage, but anyone who has would have no reason to dismiss Olaus's monsters so quickly.

Instead of narwhals, we saw plenty of its closest relative: the beluga, an animal in general far more social and visible. And while its name has none of the foreboding of its horned cousin, the beluga is a similar color as the narwhal, and the pods that swam by us bore the color of the bloated corpses of mariners, breaching the surface as they migrated by in the dozens. Who's to say what Magnus Olaus would have seen in such a spectacle, and who's to say to what degree he'd have been wrong?

"Between the printing of Olaus's 1539 *Carta Marina* and the 1555 *History*," Nigg writes, "modern zoology was being born, and with it the observation and classification of marine life." As such, he argues, Olaus straddles two intellectual worlds, relying both on Pliny and other classical authorities, and on direct observation and personal testimony. "His commentaries on individual animals are a blend of scholarship, oral tradition, and personal experience"; in being "sometimes misguided, contradictory, and confusing," Nigg concludes, they "clearly indicate the fluid nature of natural history." The accuracy of his cartography is unimportant; he produced an anthology of natural history, folktales, and myths, all told spatially rather than chronologically, a mixture of methodologies (sociology, geography, literature, history) synthesized into a single unified representation like a time-lapse photograph.

The perfect map — the map I wanted with me in the Arctic, one that was faithful to geography while still preserving the sense of wonder and mythology of a map like Olaus's — is of course an impossibility. Borges, in his short story "On Exactitude in Science," has an empire's cartographers conceive of a perfect map, one whose size is the same as the empire's, and which conforms to it point for point. Perfect, but meaningless:

> The following Generations, who were not so fond of the Study of Cartography as their Forebears had been, saw that that vast Map was Useless, and not without some Pitilessness was it that they delivered it up to the Inclemencies of Sun and Winters. In the Deserts of the West, still today, there are Tattered Ruins of the Map, inhabited by Animals and Beggars; in all the Land there is no other Relic of the Disciplines of Geography.

And that map, after all, was purely geographic — how much more difficult would it be to add layers of fantasy and the grotesque, of the evolution of human knowledge, all on the same plane?

A map must begin by excluding things, rather than attempting to bring everything in. The map we are most accustomed to in the West is the Mercator Projection, often accused of not only being wrong, but also of perpetuating a European, Anglocentric bias. While the map is almost perfectly accurate at the equator, as it moves toward the poles it becomes increasingly distorted. With the northern Atlantic at the center of the world, Africa appears smaller than Asia, the tip of Russia is cut off, and southern latitudes are blurred and downplayed altogether. But to be fair, the Mercator projection was not designed with any of this in mind — its primary function was to guide sailors from Europe to America and back; its full name is in fact *Nova et Aucta Orbis Terrae Descriptio ad Usum Navigantium Emendata*: "New and Augmented Description of Earth Corrected for the Use of Sailors." In this regard it is actually quite useful, even elegant: it represents lines of constant bearing, or "rhumb lines," as straight lines, simplifying navigation immensely. To translate the world into such a useful order is not easy.

The danger lies in taking such a projection for reality. Any map will illuminate certain elements of the earth, while at the same time distorting, or erasing others altogether. The land is the raw material, unchanging. But any map can highlight some new feature that didn't exist before, while blotting out features on another. With multiple maps you can gradually attain a more synthetic picture, or you can rely on a single projection that misrepresents the actual world around you. What you cannot do, what Borges's mapmakers tried to do, is to get everything onto one plane of paper.

Borges's parable appears, among many places, in Alessandro Scafi's *Maps of Paradise,* a work that offers yet a different way of reading maps. Scafi's book follows two millennia of cartographic attempts to locate the biblical paradise on the earth, Paradise — a word that may evolved from the ancient Medes term *para-daiza,* "a place enclosed with a clay wall," and which the Greek writer Xenophon described as a hunting park for the elite — was for centuries assumed to be a physical space, and thus to be placed on any serious map. The decisions about its location reflected mapmakers' attitudes toward time, space, and how we map them.

Medieval maps, for example, put Asia at the top of the map, with Europe and the Mediterranean, in far more detail, in the middle, and Africa and the Atlantic crammed into the bottom. Giovanni Leardo's 1442 map of the world, for example, is bisected between left and right along an axis that runs from the Indian Ocean at the top to the Sea of Spain at the bottom. To the left is Europe, or at least southern Europe; everything above the Alps is jammed into a flat band of mountain and blank space. To the right is North Africa, which gives way to a giant Red Sea, painted red. In Leardo's map, Jerusalem is at the dead center of the world, and at the top of the map, in distant, unreachable Asia, is the Garden of Eden.

Medieval maps represented the Garden of Eden as real, but inaccessible. Always located in Asia, it was far past mountains and rivers — theoretically possible, but practically unreachable. These mapmakers, Scafi notes,

> did not deploy a universal system of map signs arranged in mathematical order, but depicted neighboring places and events next to each other, without concern for the exact distance or direction between them. To them the crucial factor in the structure and content of *mappae mundi* was history, not geography.

Like Olaus's *Carta Marina,* these maps were not the result of shoddy cartography, but of a different set of priorities. "A medieval *mappa mundi* is far more than a spatial facsimile of the earth such as *Google Earth,*" Scafi writes:

> [T]he incorporation of paradise on medieval world maps, far from being a naïve depiction of some picturesque fantasy land, epitomised a vital element of Christian doctrine. The Garden of Eden signified far more than a mythical state of innocence or fanciful dreamland, forever lost. The earthly paradise pointed to a present and future reality, that of Christian redemption.

This general worldview changed only after the Protestant Reformation. Luther argued that Paradise had disappeared from the earthly world after the Fall; accordingly, it began to disappear from maps from the 16th century onward. Additionally, it was harder to contain both time *and* space on the same map; as cultures put more emphasis on commerce, and thus navigation, maps had less to do with the earthly paradise. East was no longer the top of the map, and maps began to assume the shape that we now take to be automatic: a purely functional description of the land with no regard to history, theology, or myth.

⁓

In *Arctic Dreams* Lopez writes of the maps he used in the Arctic Circle, how he traveled everywhere with them despite the fact that none of them were ever truly accurate. "They were the projection," he writes, "of a wish that the space could be this well organized." Up near the poles, traditional projections are so ill-suited, and distortion so extreme, that the Arctic seems destined to be captured only in incomplete and unreliable maps. Even as the rest of the world is becoming increasingly overlaid with more and more maps — thanks to Google and others endlessly collecting, mining, cataloging, aggregating, and analyzing data — the Arctic remains immune. The land around Svalbard is in a very specific sense useless, without much commercial or national value. When Svalbard was an active whaling and mining destination, there were attempts to map this land — charting locations of whales and seams of coal — but all that is mostly finished, and land is left now mainly to tourists like myself, and what maps we have are full of empty, white space.

The Arctic is a place where the traditional rules of topography seem not to apply. Heading up the northwest coast of the archipelago, a horde of fulmars congregated one day in our wake. I had thought perhaps that the cook had thrown some scraps of food overboard, but I was told instead that when fulmars are hatched they follow the rivers to the ocean, and that these birds were now confusing our white wake in the ocean as another river, one they vainly tried to follow.

It's not as though we expect any longer to do without GPS, sonar, and any other means at our disposal, particularly in open sea or trapped in dense fog, when a traveler of course becomes appreciative of finely detailed, stubbornly pragmatic maps — maps designed not for dreaming but for navigation. But as a mere passenger on that ship, I found myself longing for something like a bastard combination of Olaus's map and a medieval *mappa mundi*, a map into which I could read more than just topography, but also history, culture, myth, the slow evolution of the natural world. A map that would contain not just actual rivers but all the false and temporary rivers like that of our boat's wake, that the fulmars took to be as real as anything. ⚏

39, 2010
GELATIN-SILVER PRINT, 10" X 8"

ISR2, 2001
PHOTOGRAM ON CHROMOGENIC PAPER
24" X 20"

0696, 2006
INKJET PRINT
33 3/4" X 50 1/2"

STUDIO MIRROR, 2011, INKJET PRINT, 42" X 28"

BARN DOOR, TOWN FARM, SIMSBURY, CT, 2003
CHROMOGENIC PRINT
12" X 15"

DAYLIGHT, 1994
INKJET PRINT
27" X 34"

BAMBOO, 2003
SELENIUM-TONED GELATIN-SILVER PRINT
18" X 22"

LA-C 135, 1977-78
GELATIN-SILVER CONTACT PRINT
4 3/4" X 3 3/4"

FACING:
9345, 2009
INKJET PRINT
32 5/8" X 21 5/8"

16, 2012
INKJET PRINT
51" X 40"

XIV, 1988
POLACOLOR ER PRINT
24" X 19 1/2"

LUCIAN FREUD, *SLEEPING BY THE LION CARPET*, 1996, OIL ON CANVAS
(1922-2011) / PRIVATE COLLECTION
PHOTO CREDIT: © THE LUCIAN FREUD ARCHIVE / THE BRIDGEMAN ART LIBRARY

LUCIEN AND SIGMUND: THINKING IN PICTURES

GEORGE PROCHNIK

"Unquestionably older than the latter both
ontogenetically and phylogenetically."

— SIGMUND FREUD

Lucian Freud liked to say that he admired his grandfather most as a zoologist. "Lucian's passion, absolute passion, for animals, even dead animals," observed the Picasso biographer John Richardson, "like having a stuffed zebra head and dead chickens and things, all that came straight from Sigmund." Animals were always part of the painter's repertoire of portrait subjects. Dogs, horses, rats, monkeys, cats, birds — both on their own and in the company of humans — appear everywhere in his canvases. He always lived in the midst of a menagerie as well. He'd loved horses since childhood, rode them, and sometimes slept in the stable under the same blanket with them, resolving early on to be a jockey if he couldn't be a painter. Dogs were constant companions, and, especially as he grew older, his own face came increasingly to resemble the elongated countenance, at once pointed and willowy, of his whippet, Pluto. He cuddled foxes on occasion. Within the walls of his different homes and studio spaces there were, at times, sparrowhawks, kestrels, and other birds of prey. His own hard stare was compared to that of a winged predator.

After Lucian Freud took over his grandfather's home in Hampstead, Stephen Spender rented the attic apartment of four rooms, the largest of which he let Lucian use as his studio, a space the painter filled with dead birds. Geordie Greig, in his shamelessly distracted, potpourri biography, *Breakfast with Lucian: The Astounding Life and Outrageous Times of Britain's Great Modern Painter*, recounts the surreal backstory to a famous photograph depicting Lucian Freud in bed, looking like winter, primevally ancient, while Kate Moss curls around him from the side — high summer personified, sated and golden. A director making a movie about Lucian in his 86th year had brought a wild zebra into her film studio for the painter to ride, as a playful allusion to the recurrent depictions of these animals in his paintings. When Lucian tapped the zebra on the nose and the zebra broke loose, the painter gripped the reins and wouldn't let go. The zebra threw him to the floor, then pulled him across the studio. David Dawson, Lucian's longtime assistant, thought it would be the end of him. He was hurried to the emergency room. The shot of Moss entwined about Freud was taken while he was recuperating in the hospital from being dragged along a studio floor by the zebra.

Freud was drawn to something feral in Moss's own nature as well, which is why in her case he made an exception to his rule of not working with professional models. The restaurateur Jeremy King recounted that Freud spoke of Moss exactly as he talked about foxes. "He liked the free spirit. He liked the bite of danger," King asserted.

But while Freud's interest in the frisson of danger was real, his fascination with animals, both wild and domesticated, went deeper, calling to mind his grandfather's explanation, in a letter to Marie Bonaparte, for his own attraction to the canine tribe: "Dogs love their friends and bite their enemies, quite unlike people, who are incapable of pure love and always have to mix love and hate in their object relations." The idea of pure feeling obsessed both men. For Sigmund, the impossibility of actualizing pure emotion lay at the root of human suffering. In Lucian's case, the embodiment of such feeling remained a real aspiration.

The profound connection between these two observers of humanity was hinted at by a snarky online comment posted in the *Daily Mail* about one of Lucian's best-known paintings, a nude portrait of an immense woman nestled on a threadbare couch. "*Benefits Supervisor Sleeping*, is the reason why clothes are the world's greatest invention," went the wisecrack. In the sense that clothing helps us to obscure our true nature, Lucian might have agreed. Discussing the challenge of painting nudes with Michael Auping in an interview reproduced for the finely executed catalog of *Lucian Freud: Portraits*, an exhibition at the National Portrait Gallery in London and the Modern Art Museum of Fort Worth, Lucian noted, "There is, in effect, nothing to be hidden. You are stripped of your costume."

The painter's distaste for disguise extended to cosmetics. After speaking with one heavily made-up woman, he protested, "I felt I couldn't see who I was talking to." This bias resonates with Lucian's confession that "I am inclined to think of 'humans' […] if they're dressed, as animals dressed up." More indicative was his claim to be only "really interested in people as animals […] I like people to look as natural and as physically at ease as animals, as Pluto, my whippet."

In another portrait of Sue Tilley, the enormous woman of *Benefits Supervisor Sleeping* (which set a record price, at $33.6 million, for a painting by a living artist), Freud made such associations explicit. For the vertical composition, *Sleeping by the Lion Carpet*, Tilley is depicted slumbering in a brown armchair, her head fallen to one side, her left arm draped over a colossal thigh, her right hand twisted up and back to prop her face, cheek squished into her palm. A large figural carpet, elevated off the floor so that it covers the studio wall behind her, shows a pair of lions stalking a group of gazelles. Tilley's form seems to belong to this fantastical wild habitat, with its lush indigo sky and tawny hides, in some far more substantial fashion than to the dull gray-brown floor at her bare feet. Indeed, her head is positioned in such a way that it might almost be painted into the carpet, just beneath the lower lion, which is crouched, preparing to spring. She might also be construed as dreaming the primeval background scene that frames her face, her closed eyes screening the final moment before the hunt becomes a kill.

Often Freud's models would end up sitting for him for over a hundred hours in a process that could last many months, sometimes years. Embarrassment about the way one looks falls away under the glare of so prolonged a stare. Not all the emotions that replace it need be desirable, but that particular, red-faced register of being on display must begin to dissolve before Freud could paint. He believed that, in the end, the sitter's pose evolved to reflect his or her own foundational identity.

In *Man with a Blue Scarf*, the critic Martin Gayford's quietly enlightening account of sitting for two portraits by Lucian Freud over the period of a year and a half, Freud's commitment to shamelessness, both in his own life and in the self-manifestation of his sitters, crops up repeatedly. Freud plainly relished unsettling others with anecdotes of his days in Paddington in the 1950s when a number of his friends, neighbors, and subjects were criminals. He expressed mild contempt for those of his pals, like Stephen Spender, who prized the standard virtues and wanted to be liked. "Better than wanting to be disliked, perhaps," Gayford countered. "My idea was always to be feared," Freud responded. His underworld companions robbed banks, slashed their enemies' faces with razors stuck in potatoes, and doped dogs at racetracks. "I thought that was really clever and imaginative," Freud noted of the last crime. At one point Freud remarked to Gayford of a mutual painter friend, "He has a quality that only the very best people and the very worst have, he's absolutely shameless."

Clearly, Freud enjoyed the tingle of shocking expectations, but he also knew just how far he could go before real alienation kicked in. You don't end up leaving a £96 million will as Freud did — the largest sum ever bequeathed by a British artist — having lived in radical defiance of *all* social rules. Greig registers Freud's deft navigation of English society but leaves it unanalyzed. A materialist study of Freud's career has yet to be written but could prove more revealing than all the googly-eyed reiterations of his famed "Lothario" propensities.

In any event, freedom from shame was something that sitting for Freud could, at least temporarily, impart to sitters as a kind of therapeutic side effect. Tilley reported how her initial nervousness about stripping before Freud was short-lived. She soon grew used to being naked before the artist, and this familiarity was complemented by a sense of falling in love with the painting Freud was creating of her. "I'm not the 'ideal woman,' I know I'm not," Tilley later said. "But who is? And he never made the skinny ones look any better. He picks out every single detail."

The fantasy vision of the painter's studio as a place where every sitter is seen fully, through and through, constitutes a radically egalitarian realm. The person who can see *all* our flaws — every last quirk of our fleshly being — would come to understand these defects so completely, and place them in so wide a context, that they would cease to be stigmas. Refusing the fetishistic focus on a single grotesque trait, the perception of ugliness would come full circle to where awareness of beauty is regained. In this way, Freud's studio had the quality of a dream tribunal at which the defendant accused of dreadful things is given space to lay out with unlimited expansiveness the ways that he or she is not the monster depicted by the prosecution, but so much more besides and something else entirely. Freud enjoined his sitters to do nothing but be, in his words, "punctual, patient and nocturnal," while holding nothing back in the visual confession they made before him of their physical being.

The illuminating effect of shedding shame and self-consciousness could work both ways for painter and model. Speaking of *Benefits Supervisor Sleeping*, Freud told an interviewer that he'd initially been "very aware of all kinds of spectacular things to do with her size, like amazing craters and things one's never seen before." But over time, as Sarah Howgate notes in a perceptive essay for the *Portraits* exhibition catalog, Tilley "became more ordinary to him." In place of the spectacular, he came to recognize the intense persistence of Tilley's essential femininity. Freud acknowledged being drawn to extravagant bodies and, as much as he mistrusted this predilection in himself, continued to seek them out as a kind of testing ground for his powers of concentration, striving to see through the temptation of physically sensational features to the ur-forms preserved beneath their monumental rolls.

"You must make judgments about the painting, but not about the subject," Freud once stated. Such an attitude requires striving to see past any single feature of the sitter in isolation, even if that trait is ravishing. In his book, Greig asks the painter, "And with the portraits of Caroline [Blackwood], were her enormous luminous eyes what was important?" "I never really think of features by themselves," Freud rejoins. "It is about the presence." The answer correlates with what Gayford calls Freud's lack of sympathy for references to people having, for example, appealing eyes, legs, or busts. "I would have thought that if you wanted to be with someone, you would find *everything* about them erotic," Freud remarked to Gayford. For the period of the sitting, anyway, Freud wanted to be with all his subjects, and this communicated powerfully to them. One model observed that posing for him "felt like being an apple in the Garden of Eden. When it was over, I felt as if I had been cast out of Paradise."

But what, then, ends up on display for the viewer? What happens when the depth of dialogue between painter and sitter has enabled the artist to break through easy, socially conditioned responses to the human physique in order to portray some more fundamental quality than the labels "beautiful" and "ugly" typically suggest? These questions point to others about the nature of Freud's art. He's regularly characterized as a masterful realist painter, but that label may obscure more than it elucidates. If we're studied as relentlessly as Freud purportedly observed his subjects, is the image on the canvas necessarily more objective? Or does the hypertrophied focus and temporal extension of the gaze mean that the rendering of the subject must then reflect the seer's own psychological landscape? "My work is purely autobiographical," Freud once announced. "It is about myself and my surroundings. It is an attempt at a record. I work from the people that interest me and that I care about, in rooms that I live in and know. I use the people to invent my pictures with, and I can work more freely when they are there."

And what about all those moments in Freud's work where elements of the surreal blatantly intrude into the realist frame, as in the painting that shows a naked man nursing a swaddled infant, while in the foreground an older man calmly reads a book with a gray dog curled at his feet? Or the early interior, *The Painter's Room*, in which an enormous red and yellow zebra head juts through a square-cut window in a blue wall to hover above a tattered couch, evocative of the psychoanalytic patient's lying-place? Or the portrait of a naked man in a weak contrapposto pose on a draped bed embracing a whippet, while another set of legs identical to those of the subject emerges from under the bedcovers along the floorboards?

The realist label for Freud's work seems to correspond with his professed intention to make paint "work as flesh." The thick, textured, dimensionality of his mottled oils is epidermal, to be sure. But something mystical creeps in when Freud appends to this aspiration the wish that his portraits "be *of* the people, not *like* them. Not having a look of the sitter, *being* them." The label becomes more suspect still when we probe the question of what the reality of flesh consists in. While Freud talks of his intention to depict just what he sees, he elsewhere says, "The artist who tries to serve nature is only an executive artist." To Gayford he expressed distaste for Picasso's wish to make paintings that "amaze, surprise and astonish." In remarks for the catalog of an exhibition he curated of favorite paintings by other artists he asserted, "What do I ask of a painting? I ask it to astonish, disturb, seduce, convince." Often Freud talked of despising paintings that exhibit theatrical propensities. Yet, in conversation with Auping, he mused that his painting was "a kind of unconscious theater. In an ancient world, painting and theater would probably be considered very close," Freud opined.

Whatever else, his paradoxical comments reinforce the impression of artistic ambitions aimed backward toward the borders of myth, bent on evoking those primordial figures and configurations that spawned humanity's mythic vision. It's true, as well, that both Freud and his sitters commented on the "prophetic" character of his portraits — specifically the way he seemed, on occasion, to inscribe the imminence of death, self- or time-inflicted, on the lineaments of his models' features. The writer and heiress Caroline Blackwood, who was once Freud's lover and model, noted grimly that the eyes of his sitters as they gaze out from his portraits "suggest that, like the blind Tiresias, they have 'foresuffered all.'"

<hr />

Another sensation tendered by the experience of sitting for Freud was release from consciousness of time. In part this was due to the sheer magnitude of the temporal commitment to which each model agreed. How could sitters have continued to tick off minutes when they knew the sessions might ultimately consume 150 hours or more of their existence? That trademark woe of our age — pointless freneticism, the ricochet between communication devices and actual communication — had to be let go in Freud's studio. His attitude, as he conveyed it to Gayford, was the reverse of working to a deadline. "When one is doing something to do with quality, even a lifetime doesn't seem enough," Freud maintained.

By virtue of his eccentric personality, Freud seemed able to create an atmosphere that displaced sitters as well from the customary axes of their lives. Gayford described his hours modeling for Freud as "remorselessly intimate," in a manner that bore affinities to marriage, crowding out other friendships and responsibilities. "It is an experience almost like returning to youth, endless time and nothing to do, for the sitter at least, except chat," Gayford wrote. "I'm not sure whether it is filling a hole in my life, but it is enthralling." Elsewhere he likens the experience of posing for Freud to meditation, a comparison that resonates with his daughter Bella's observation that the attendant break from daily routine "makes you conscious of life going on in the nicest way possible."

Needless to say, the economic reality of interrupting mundane life required, at the least, a flexible work schedule. Though Freud often paid his sitters something — on occasion with an etching of the oil portrait he was painting of them — many of his models were well able to afford their time off from rote being. Mostly, he compensated subjects with his own dashingly entertaining conversation and by cooking them fancy game or lobster dinners accompanied by champagne — repasts that factored as part of the painting process.

Gayford observes that journalism — his own profession — does not require sustained effort, but "can be done on a rush of adrenaline, then on to the next thing. Maybe that's what's the matter with it," he muses. "Watching LF paint my portrait is making me think about the way I work myself. It is an example, enacted before my eyes at every sitting, of measured, steady progress towards a final goal." This steadiness in no way precludes discursion; rather, such attention, again like meditation, enlarges his field of vision, allowing him to understand the context for his undertaking. Lucian also had a kind of spiritual reverence for the relationship between his subjects and their larger setting. "I like the models to be around in the studio even when I am painting something else," he once said. "They seem to change the atmosphere, in the same way that saints do, by their presence."

ANIMAL MUMMIES, CATS: ROMAN PERIOD, 1st CENTURY AD, LONDON, BRITISH MUSEUM
FROM *HISTORY OF EGYPT* BY J.H. BREASTED

The particular sense in Lucian's subjects of having been granted dispensation to detach and unwind from the contours of habitual behavior evokes, as well, the world of Sigmund Freud's consulting room. There, too, for months or years on end, analysands positioned in a state of repose allowed that which was hidden deep within to be slowly coaxed into visibility, or at least audibility. The precisely choreographed room where Sigmund saw patients — evocatively lit, mysteriously arrayed with antiquities, muted, secluded from the outside world — made for a chamber where patients' fantasies and dreams felt at home, able to emerge and become subject to the doctor's verbal dissection. Gayford describes Lucian Freud's studio as a kind of operating theater, constructed in relationship to light so as to allow sitters to be viewed from multiple angles in the most controlled, revealing manner possible. Lucian's demeanor while painting resembled that of "an explorer or hunter in some dark forest," Gayford writes.

But what, finally, do these loose parallels between the practice of the doctor and the artist signify? To speak of a release from shame and time as therapeutic benefits is not to imply that these rewards were ever intended as such by the artist himself. No one — Lucian least of all — ever pretended that the experience of posing for him was meant to be in the service of anything but his painting. Why, then, was it in Lucian's own interest for his subjects to enter into an unselfconscious meditative state analogous to that which Sigmund Freud sought to engender in patients? What, finally, is the relationship between the two men's endeavors, and what can we learn from considering them in conjunction?

HORUS FALCON, BASALT, C. 600 BCE, PARIS
FROM *HISTORY OF EGYPT* BY J.H. BREASTED

An intriguing link between the two men can be traced through the work of James H. Breasted, an American Egyptologist. Breasted, who participated in the excavation of King Tutankhamun's tomb and became one of the world's foremost archeologists, was also a respected scholar of the ancient world. When the German-language version of his history of Egypt was published in the 1930s, in an edition rich with color plates and line illustrations, it became the standard work in Germany and Austria, where the discipline of archeology held exalted stature. Sigmund Freud considered Breasted's work "authoritative" and drew on it in his own research into the evolution of human psychology.

Lucian Freud was presented with a copy of this same book when he turned 16 in 1939, and the volume remained a reference point, inspiration, and portrait subject in its own right throughout his life. He made two portraits and an etching of the book open beside a gray pillow, as well as a painting of his mother reading the work. No other book is so featured in the painter's work.

The frontispiece of Breasted's *Geschichte Aegyptens* (*History of Egypt*) presents a color photo of a bird of prey figurine. Turning the pages, one encounters a striking panoply of human portraits, along with lions, cats, gazelles, baboons, and mythic hybrid creatures, like sphinxes. It's easy to conceive how the artist, young and old, would find the book transfixing. But in the three portraits where the book's open pages are legible, Freud always shows the same two-plate spread depicting a pair of plaster portrait heads from the workshop of the sculptor Thutmose at Amarna. Sarah Howgate

85

SMALL SCULPTURES, LATE 18TH DYNASTY, BERLIN. FROM *HISTORY OF EGYPT* BY J.H. BREASTED

has pointed out how these twin portraits resemble two small unfinished self-portraits by Lucian, which are propped side by side against a wall in the background of his painting *Two Irishmen in W11.* The flaking, granular quality of paint in Freud's final work, *Portrait of a Hound*, a nude portrait of his assistant, Dawson, beside a whippet whose hindquarters are dissolving into blank space, is also eerily suggestive of the texture of plaster in the Egyptian heads. Speculating on why the pair of ancient portraits were so important to Lucian, Gayford notes that the Egyptians in this era created the "earliest great portraits" still extant. They are "wonderful representations of specific individuals," he adds, and perhaps as such were understood by Lucian as "representations of pure being."

Along with the history of Egypt, a second work by Breasted also proved seminal to Sigmund Freud's thinking. Breasted's *The Dawn of Conscience* was, in fact, the single greatest influence on Freud's last major essay, the controversial *Moses and Monotheism.* Breasted's book makes the argument that conscience — and, arguably, human consciousness as such — originated, not as Biblical sources contend among the Hebrews, but within Egyptian society during the brief, revolutionary reign of Amenhotep. Amenhotep, Freud wrote (following Breasted), developed a religion with marked similarities to early Judaism, most notably in its swerve from a universal god or gods to exclusivist monotheism. Sigmund dates the start of Amenhotep's rule to about 1375 BCE and quotes Breasted's reference to this pharaoh as "the first individual in human history." *Moses and Monotheism*, published in 1937, used Breasted's arguments about Amenhotep's character to make the case that Moses was by blood an Egyptian who'd been heavily influenced by that ruler and left Egypt after Amenhotep's death to found his own religion.

Freud's motivations for writing this work, which was castigated for depriving the Jews of their heroic lawgiver right at the outbreak of World War II, were complex. But critics of Freud's book tend to overlook the extreme ambivalence of the doctor's portrait of Amenhotep. On the one hand, per Breasted, Freud designated him as history's first individual. However, Amenhotep was also responsible, Freud argued, for bringing Egyptian religion "greater clarity, consistency, harshness, and intolerance." Freud himself was never a monotheist, and in 1939 the decision to create a revisionist genealogy of the charismatic founder of a harsh, intolerant faith was hardly a simple paean to moral genius. Freud's interest in tracing Moses's roots reflected his concern with trying to excavate the psychological situation that gave birth to human conscience — a moment which also might be said to mark the appearance of the first "symptom" from which all subsequent human neuroses evolved. While conscience was essential for the survival of civilization, it also represented for Freud the disease that no one "civilized" could ever truly recover from.

It's not coincidental that the double-page spread in the Egyptian book which Lucian received the same year his grandfather published *Moses and Monotheism* — the two portraits that he paints again and again — are dated to precisely the period that struck his grandfather as foundational for the human predicament. The head on the left is dated to around 1400 BCE, the head on the right to 1370 BCE. According to his grandfather's dating scheme, they thus perfectly span the period just before and after Amenhotep's assumption of power, tracking between them the dawn of human conscience and individual consciousness. Lucian Freud was obsessed with "the individuality of absolutely everything," Gayford reports, not just people and animals, but eggs and other objects as well. At the same time, he had a phobia about being photographed and a devout hatred of activities he perceived as efforts either to conceal or counterfeit people's biological identity.

TITAN, *DIANA AND CALLISTO*, 1556-1559, OIL ON CANVAS, 74" X 18.5"

Lucian described himself, indeed, on more than one occasion as a biologist, explaining that he liked to paint nudes because of the way the naked body served as a translucent window onto forms that lay deeper underneath. "One of the most exciting things is seeing through the skin, to the blood and veins and markings," he remarked to the art critic William Feaver. Above all, Lucian used his vision, his understanding of selfhood as something distinct from the usual confluence of ego and identity, to make the case for a kind of animal individuality. As Marina Warner once noted, Lucian was a determinist who "paradoxically managed to restore to the naked body its character as the inalienable possession of an individual."

Yet if both Sigmund and Lucian felt driven to look backward to a moment when the human countenance could still express "pure," biologically defined being, their rationale for doing so was ostensibly antithetical. Whereas Sigmund's psychoanalytic project was, in theory, dedicated to helping people become more conscious as a way of helping them acquire a measure of perspective and control over their drives, Lucian was interested in returning his subjects — or at least their bodies — to the depths of unconsciousness. While his grandfather studded his consulting room with ancient figurines from Egypt, Greece, and Rome as totemic spirits that might catalyze the analytic process of exorcism, tempting the patient's incubi to emerge by way of sympathetic identification, we might say that Lucian Freud sought to transform his subjects back into those ancient dream-beings from which modern human psychology evolved.

Once again, what all this means for viewers of Lucian's canvases is, of course, debatable. What would appear in a portrait that actually succeeded in depicting pure being? In Lucian Freud's idiom, might this ideal represent the point at which our most archaic selves and absolute individuality converge? If the painter's true aspirations, in life and art both, were aimed at getting beyond the symptom of conscience, what are we left with but raw id? Caroline Blackwood, who knew well what it felt like to be painted by Lucian, to be both intimate with him and sexually betrayed by him, and to drive him out of his mind and into a state of pure anguish when she'd left him, once wrote, "Lucian Freud has always had the ability to make the people and objects that come under his scrutiny seem more themselves, and more *like* themselves, than they have ever been — or likely will be." In this richly enigmatic observation we glimpse the start of an answer to many questions raised here.

Blackwood implies that a painting might so far transgress the boundaries of mere semblance as to literally reconstitute an aspect of the subject's reality that the subject herself has surrendered to social constructs. In so doing, she hints at a third form of delivery conjured in Freud's studio. But to chart this last release we must first consider a pair of Titian paintings that Lucian called the most beautiful pictures in the world.

Both paintings, *Diana and Actaeon* and *Diana and Callisto* (1556–1559), portray mythological scenes involving a fatal exposure of flesh. Each canvas shows a human subject unwittingly contracting sexual guilt in the eyes of the virgin-huntress goddess, Diana. In *Diana and Actaeon*, Actaeon is represented accidentally stumbling into the scene of Diana bathing naked with her handmaidens; Diana's gaze is furious as she tries to veil herself from Actaeon's helpless stare. In *Diana and Callisto*, Diana commands her own nymphs to expose the nakedness of her handmaiden Callisto, thereby baring proof of her illicit pregnancy (caused, in fact, by rape). Sexuality as such has doomed these human beings. Titian shows the figures in the instant before Diana moves to punish them.

"These Titians [...] have what every good picture has to have, which is a little bit of poison," Lucian remarked. "In the case of a painting the poison cannot be isolated and diagnosed as it could be in food. Instead, it might take the form of an attitude. A sense of mortality could be the poison in a picture, as it is in these."

But the sense of death pervading these canvases is only part of what gives them their aura of luminous, perilous imminence. Those who know their myths as Freud did will recall that, before being torn apart, Actaeon is transformed into a stag. Callisto, before dying, is turned into a bear, then set amid the stars. Both figures, driven to violate the rule of a god by virtue of an erotic nature for which they bear no responsibility, are changed into beasts.

Finally, we might conjecture that what Lucian Freud sought to portray in his profoundly disturbing, riveting canvases, was a form of emancipation from the human condition as such — the release of metamorphosis. The dream life of flesh is all made up of animals, the painter suggests. His grandfather, meditating on the collapse of European civilization in the late 1930s while reading Breasted's history of Egypt, would have agreed. Ultimately, more even than trying to imbue the individual with knowledge that allowed control over the drives, Sigmund, like Lucian, sought to bare those animal truths that damn man's efforts to deify himself, locating truth and beauty closer to the bone.

In the fall of 2013, Vienna's Kunsthistorisches Museum mounted the city's first exhibition of Lucian Freud's paintings. Throughout his lifetime, Freud persistently refused invitations from Viennese curators to display his work, refusing to exonerate the Austrian state from culpability in his family's fate. Among the portraits on display in the posthumous show is a work depicting his lover Bernardine Coverley sinking into an old, dark, Freudian couch, face averted, breasts engorged, pregnant with the future in the form of their daughter, Bella. She's pure physicality — but enlarged rather than reduced by that containment within the body. On the label is a note reading: "This painting is exhibited in memory of Sigmund Freud's sisters, who were deported from Vienna and died in concentration camps: Rosa in Auschwitz, Mitzi in Theresienstadt, Dolfi and Paula in Treblinka." The anonymous tribute in this haunted setting evokes a line Freud scrawled in charcoal over the densely paint-gobbed walls of his studio: "Art is escape from personality." ⁄⁄

ABOVE: GREEN SLATE TABLET
FIRST DYNASTY, CIRCA 3400 BCE
OXFORD, ASHMOLEAN MUSEUM
FROM *HISTORY OF EGYPT* BY J.H. BREASTED.

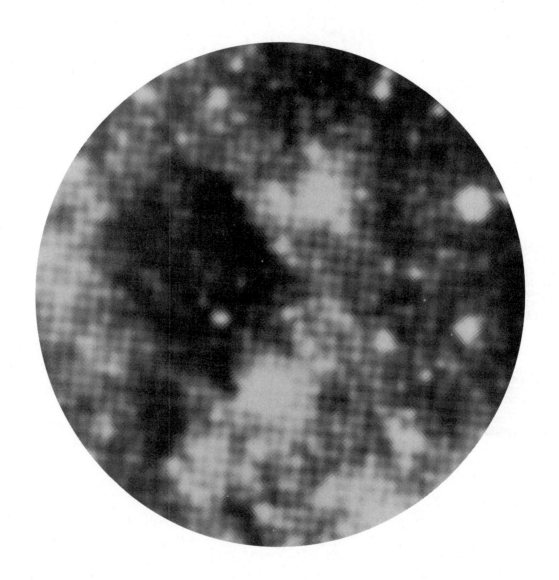

Post-Verdict Renga for Trayvon

LAUREN K. ALLEYNE

Provincetown, MA

Heat. Bodies gleaming with sweat and sun.
Day pressing itself against everything:
unforgiving. I am walking down this street
thinking of another walk in another city,
of a boy who never makes it home. I, too,
am armed with thirst and a craving for
sweetness; I, too, wear his brown skin
and do not belong here, to this city
of leisure and narrow streets. Fear
passes through me, a phantom, and is
gone. Overhead, flags flutter in the
thick, salty air. *Not guilty*, they say.
Not guilty. Not guilty. Not guilty.
Not guilty. Not guilty.

Beginning is red—
a door, a car, the bowed lips,
a nameless flower.

*

I have so few names for things
here, I fall into silence

Two men, black as God,
their shirts golden as morning.
No words between us.

*

So much passes in the glance
that the throat cannot muster.

Three headless torsos
in a store window. A light
trick makes men of them.

*

In this city of flesh, you
can almost forget the ghosts.

Fat daylilies crown
long green stalks, their orange heads
the color of grief.

*

No candlelight vigils here
only the living, living.

He walks, oak brown, bald,
belly like a commandment—
I am here: make way

*

Nothing I say will save you,
but how can I say nothing?

Thick black curls cut close,
buttoned black shirt. Caramel face
diamonded with sweat.

*

A dark, ageless face
wise and innocent as earth—
how have you survived?

I can't stop counting
the bodies that look like yours:
five this whole morning.

*

I can't say if this matters,
just that I saw, I did see.

AMANDA ROSS-HO, *RAG QUILT #1*, 2012
STUDIO RAGS, ACRYLIC AND LATEX PAINT, THREAD
SEWN BY GINA ROSS
51" X 51"
COURTESY OF THE ARTIST
PHOTO CREDIT: ROBERT WEDEMEYER

WORK, ENCOURAGEMENT, TRAVEL

JACK PENDARVIS

Work

Hired a young couple to push me around in my wheelbarrow.
They're not a couple, but I'd like to see them get together.
I'd like to fix them up. Maybe they'll bond over how much
they hate pushing me around in my wheelbarrow.

Encouragement

I think about all the encouragement I've received over the
years. Are people just being friendly? Or do they hate me?

Travel

I'll never forget the first time Bill saw the Mississippi River.
He said, "Who cares? ⫽

JOHNNY HARRIS, 2013

TRANSLATIONS FROM THE BONE–HOUSE:
On the Poetry of Seamus Heaney and John Hollander

M.P. RITGER

"The limits of my language are the limits of my world."
—Wittgenstein

Writers are strangers. It's commonplace, nowadays, to say that a writer is always an outsider, even inside his or her own life. Language — even a first language — remains foreign; language and reality seem received. Or something like that. Some of this rhetoric has undoubtedly come down to us from Modernism, from Eliot and Pound — fragmentation instead of fluency, and so on. In fact, of the many standards that Eliot and Pound and their ilk set for their poetic descendants, the importance of translation in their poetics may be the most essential. For Pound (think of his very loose translations from the Chinese and Japanese) and Eliot (think of the multiple voices transcribed into "The Waste Land") the practice and performance of translation were the practice and performance of this self-alienation, this self-strangeness that is an essential condition of being for a modern writer.

But translators are martyrs, we think. Translators are selfless, sacrificing their time and talent in the name of another writer's work. Translation (especially of poetry) is exceedingly difficult, if not impossible, and usually profitless. Translation is seen as a service to a community of readers, or to a deserving body of work. But when it comes to poetry, the translator is most often a poet in his or her own right. What is the blowback of these translations, we might ask? Is translation as essential an aspect of contemporary poetics as it seemed to Modernist poetics? Many poets who began publishing in the shadow of High Modernism (Hughes, Bishop, Ashbery, Merwin, Heaney, Hollander) have also become accomplished translators. Two of these authors — Seamus Heaney and John Hollander — passed away in August, which left many bereft, and many baffled as to how to begin to consider their achievements.

Why not start with their translations? That is, after all, where they were most fully a stranger in the language and in themselves — and therefore, one could say, most fully a writer in the contemporary vein.

Seamus Heaney's last words before his death were a phrase in Latin, sent as a text message to his wife: *Noli timere,* "Be not afraid." His son Michael made this public; he delivered one of several eulogies for the poet and Nobel laureate at the funeral services. The phrase caused a small kerfuffle on the internet as several news outlets mistranscribed, mis-Tweeted, and misreported it (the mistake was a relatively small one: *Nolle* vs. *Noli,* infinitive vs. imperative). If the poet's last lines served to breathe a moment's life back into a "dead" language, perhaps we should not be entirely surprised — that is, in a sense, what he'd been doing for the past 47 years, since the appearance of his first collection, *Death of a Naturalist,* in 1966. Often called the most "popular" poet since Robert Frost, the gruff grace of "Famous Seamus" Heaney has long seemed a throwback to a prior age. More to the point, his genius at translating Old English into our contemporary idiom has revitalized the study of the Anglo Saxon saga *Beowulf* — one of the oldest surviving texts in the language.

For poets of Heaney's generation, in the shadow of Modernism and in an era entranced with the rising reality and rhetoric of globalization and cosmopolitanism, translation was part and parcel, an aspect of every poet's job. Think of W.S. Merwin, for example, whose translations from Spanish and French are credited in part with importing an increased awareness of the possibilities of surrealism into his own poetry, but also into the milieu of American poetry in general. Unlike Merwin, who long ago retreated to his dreamy Hawaii, Heaney was a vocal and ever-present ambassador to and from his poetic realms: Ireland and the English-speaking world, both past and present. There are other translator-poets whose contributions have been more prolific, but Heaney's relationship to translation was a special one, and especially generous — in fact, it was ideal.

In 1984 Heaney completed what was at that point his largest-scale project as a translator: a version of the medieval Irish poem *Buile Suibhne.* Heaney's "Sweeney Astray" adapted and re-presented the tale of the metamorphosed Irish king in segments of both poetry and prose, rendering with particular care the flights of lyric fancy in Sweeney's descriptions of his beloved home (an area of Ireland not far from the counties where Heaney himself grew up):

> The blackthorn is a jaggy creel
> stippled with dark sloes;
> green watercress in thatch on wells
> where the drinking blackbird goes…
>
> Low-set clumps of apple trees
> drum down fruit when shaken;
> scarlet berries clot like blood
> on mountain rowan.

On display in these translated lines are all of Heaney's own most distinctive features as a poet, and precisely what makes him such an excellent match for Old English poetry. Sharp, heavily stressed and spondaic phrases ("jaggy creel," "low-set clumps") populate the line, as strange strings of monosyllabic words jut off the page ("drum down fruit," "clot like blood"). The texture of a Seamus Heaney poem always feels physical, like "earth took of earth" (to quote another small but famous Anglo-Saxon poem). This is achieved partly through the clarity of his images, but mostly by the stressed clumps and clots of worded-sounds that make up his language:

Between my finger and my thumb
The squat pen rests; snug as a gun.

That, of course, is the beginning of "Digging," Heaney's most famous poem, which opens *Opened Ground: Selected Poems 1966–1996*. The poet's personal word-hoard has almost always seemed dragged from the Germanic, craggy reaches of the vast geography of modern English. Consider several lines from the close of another early poem, "Death of a Naturalist," for example:

Then one hot day when fields were rank
With cowdung in the grass the angry frogs
Invaded the flax-dam; I ducked through hedges
To a course croaking that I had not heard
Before. The air was thick with a bass chorus.
Right down the dam gross-bellied frogs were cocked
On sods; their loose necks pulsed like sails. Some hopped:
The slap and plop were obscene threats. Some sat
Poised like mud grenades, their blunt heads farting.

Every other word, it seems, is an onomatopoeia. The lines, strung one monosyllable after another, become extraordinarily filthy: "frogs were cocked / On sods; their loose necks pulsed like sails. Some hopped: The slap and plop." And I can't imagine anything more dazzlingly nasty than the plague of toads, "Poised like mud grenades, their blunt heads farting." Of course this endless mirroring of form and content (earthy words for rustic subjects) can also be exhausting: Susan Sontag once said that Heaney seemed to live in his own theme park, a Disney Dublin. (Then again, to be insulted by Susan Sontag is surely one of the greatest compliments of the late 20th century.)

Around the same time that his translation of *Sweeney Astray* appeared (the mid-eighties), M.H. Abrams and the editors of the *Norton Anthology of English Literature* approached Heaney about producing a fresh version of the Anglo-Saxon epic *Beowulf*. It was undoubtedly clear that Heaney's own poetic language (jagged, rough-hewn, and heavily stressed) would make him the ideal translator for the alliterative verse of Old English, though politics might have seemed to make the fit an awkward one. "Sprung from an Irish nationalist background," as

Heaney eventually wrote of himself in the introduction to his translation of *Beowulf*, "and educated at a Northern Irish Catholic school, I had learned the Irish language and lived within a cultural and ideological frame that regarded it as the language that I should by rights have been speaking but which I had been robbed of."

Though *Beowulf* is not a foundational text for England as a nation — the fact that England and its people are never even mentioned in the poem is all too easily forgotten (this is a saga about the medieval Danes and Geats, a tribe that hailed from what would now be southern Sweden) —the story is nevertheless a foundational text for the English *language*. It would seem impossible, especially for an Irishman, to separate that language from colonialism in general, or at least from linguistic colonialism. Or to forget that, as Heaney wrote in an early poem titled "Traditions," (not included in his *Selected*), "Our guttural muse / was bulled long ago / by the alliterative tradition."

A passage from Heaney's Nobel lecture poignantly illustrates his artistic and moral predicaments as an Irish artist writing himself into the tradition of English literature, and specifically during the years of the Troubles:

The child in the bedroom, listening simultaneously to the domestic idiom of his Irish home and the official idioms of the British broadcaster while picking up from behind both the signals of some other distress, that child was already being schooled for the complexities of his adult predicament, a future where he would have to adjudicate among promptings variously ethical, aesthetical, moral, political, metrical, sceptical, cultural, topical, typical, post-colonial and, taken all together, simply impossible.

Of course, and perhaps unsurprisingly, Heaney did accept the challenge of translating *Beowulf*. He had a special talent for appearing to be in the thick of a complex political issue while sidestepping it at the same time — what one might simply call being tasteful, though it was more than that. Heaney's writing was always autobiographical without being confessional, political without being didactic, and it was frequently his historical perspective that created this effect. As in the "Bog" poems, he used a broad range of historical reference to expand, not shape, his reader's understanding. This may well be the essential (and often achieved) ambition of his art: "to rhyme the contemporary with the archaic," as he said in his *Paris Review* interview.

No wonder, then, that he set himself to work on the saga, though it soon proved to be a daunting task. Despite noticing his own inherent sense for an alliterative line ("[T]he poet who had first formed my ear was Gerard Manley Hopkins," as Heaney notes in his introduction to *Beowulf*; he called Hopkins his "first love" in the *Paris Review* interview) the task was difficult on a day-to-day basis. Old English is a far, far cry from Modern English, and although he set himself a goal of completing 20 lines per day, Heaney soon felt he was "trying to bring down a megalith with a toy hammer," and let the project lapse.

What revived the translation, Heaney has told us, was that he struck upon a voice that seemed to him to match the poem's sense of self, an imagined voice that allowed his Irish identity back inside the Anglo-Saxon epic. Translation is to a greater or lesser degree always interpretation, and although the Norton editors assigned an Old English scholar as a sort of babysitter, to ensure a certain amount of accuracy, Heaney nevertheless found himself motivated by this unconventional approach, and the "erotics of composition," as he called it, became possible again. In 2000, Heaney spoke to NPR about this:

[T]his poem is written down, but it is also clearly a poem that was spoken out. And it is spoken in a very dignified, formal way. And I got the notion that the best voice I could hear it in was the voice of an old countryman who was a cousin of my father's who was not, as they say, educated, but he spoke with great dignity and formality. And I thought if I could write the translation in such a way that this man — Peter Scullion was his name — could speak it, then I would get it right. That's, in fact, how I started it.

These "big-voiced scullions," as he calls them in the introduction, gave the tone and verve to Heaney's lines. This is apparent from the get-go. Consider the very first lines of the poem:

Hwæt wē Gār-Dena   in gear-dagum
þēod-cyninga   Þrym gefrūnon,
hū þā æþelingas   ellen fremedon.

"Hwæt" is an Anglo-Saxon interjection meaning something like "Why, what! Ah!" Many of the (at least) 65 previous translators have used literary archaisms that must have seemed befitting for the introduction of an important epic poem: Lo, harken! Behold! Attend! And on and on. Now consider Heaney's version of those first lines:

So. The Spear-Danes in days gone by
and the kings who ruled them had courage and greatness.
We have heard of those prince's heroic campaigns.

Choosing "So" was motivated directly by that grand-rascal of an Irish uncle-figure that Heaney had imagined for himself. As he explains: "[I]n Hiberno-English Scullion speak, the particle 'so' […] operates as an expression that obliterates all previous discourse and narrative, and at the same time functions as an exclamation calling for immediate attention." That flat and accurate "so" called the reader's attention immediately to this forthright and plainspoken take on the complex rhythms of the Anglo-Saxon epic. Heaney makes countless of these sorts of confident compromises, where previous translators were bogged down in trying to recreate each and every poetic effect.

These poetic patterns can be extraordinarily complex. In the original, each line of Anglo-Saxon poetry is made up of two halves, split by a caesura. Each line's two halves contain two dominant stresses and are linked by their alliteration. (In the first half, both of the dominant stresses alliterate; in the second half, only the first of the two dominant stresses alliterates.) The last dominant stress in each line never alliterates, and from one line to the next, the alliterating sound never (or rarely) repeats. "So it sounds … sort of like this, / All these arduous … alliterations criss-crossing the lines," in which *so* and *sounds* link to *sort,* and *all* and *arduous* link to *alliteration.* This can be a beautiful but cumbersome sound pattern, but Heaney doesn't bawk, forging lines that are both accurate, direct, and more subtle than one might anticipate — therefore more attuned to our contemporary standards. Consider the poem's keening finish, with the hero's funeral pyre:

The Geat people built a pyre for Beowulf,
stacked and decked it until it stood foursquare,
hung with helmets, heavy war-shields
and shining armor, just as he had ordered.
Then his warriors laid him in the middle of it,
mourning a lord far-famed and beloved.

Heaney renders the Anglo-Saxon trademarks of repeated verbal phases ("stacked and decked") and of course the alliteration ("hung with helmets, heavy") but he manages this all without compromising the poem's sense or the sense of a direct address. I was lucky enough to hear Heaney recite these lines in the fall of 2012, at a reading established as a memorial for a man who had been killed in the terrorist attacks of September 11, 2001. With his characteristic grace, Heaney rededicated these lines to the memory of that man. The poem seemed then to speak directly to the grief of his friends and family:

On a height they kindled the hugest of all
funeral fires; fumes of woodsmoke
billowed darkly up, the blaze roared
and drowned out their weeping, wind died down
and flames wrought havoc in the hot bone-house,
burning it to the core. They were disconsolate
and wailed aloud for their lord's decease.
A Geat woman too sang out in grief;
with hair bound up, she unburdened herself
of her worst fears, a wild litany
of nightmare and lament: her nation invaded,
enemies on the rampage, bodies in piles,
slavery and abasement. Heaven swallowed the smoke.

As James Shapiro pointed out in *The New York Times* when the translation first appeared, it also seems impossible to read these lines without thinking of the violence of the Troubles. And now, of course, we cannot read these lines without thinking of Famous Seamus himself.

It's been said that every generation needs its own translation of the classic texts, but it seems the achievement of Heaney's *Beowulf* speaks to many, and may last longer than a generation — for an era, at least; however long that may be. In these lines, and his own, Heaney's accomplishment is "to rhyme the contemporary with the archaic." It is for this most of all that we will continue to read and remember his work. As one final example, consider the poem "Bone Dreams," from his 1975 collection *North,* in which Heaney references that classic Old English kenning for the body that appears in the description of Beowulf's funeral: *bān-hūs,* or bone-house:

In the coffered
riches of grammar
and declensions
I found *bān-hūs*,
its fire, benches,
wattle and rafter,
where the soul
fluttered a while
in the roofspace.

⸻

The poet John Hollander also passed away this August, and was also known for both his poems and for his acts of poetic embassy. Hollander's virtuosic introduction to the art, *Rhyme's Reason: A Guide To English Verse* (1981), is probably his most well-known work, and may well prove his most enduring, if only for its enshrinement in the syllabi of introductory poetry and creative writing classes. *Rhyme's Reason* is an act of inter-English translation in its own right, not only explaining what rhyme and meter are but reanimating just how some of the arcane-seeming aspects of versification work:

Iambic five-beat lines are labeled *blank*
Verse (with sometimes a foot or two reversed,
Or one more syllable—"feminine ending").
Blank verse can be extremely flexible:
It ticks and tocks the time with even feet
(Or sometimes, cleverly, can end limping).

Clever, indeed. Hollander's *Types of Shape* (1969) had taken a similar tack, embodying visual forms with his typography while demonstrating how (some) "concrete" poetry works, and harkening back to British emblematic poetry of the long 16th century (think of George Herbert's typographic experimentation in "Easter Wings"). His career as an ambassador between different stylistic and historical realms of English poetry was exemplified in his lauded work as an editor. As the steward of the Library of Congress's *American Poetry: The Nineteenth Century*, for example, Hollander was widely praised for including popular ballads and folk songs and a section on contemporaneous translations of American Indian poetry alongside the more canonical fare — Whitman, Emerson, Dickinson, Melville, Longfellow and so forth. In the world of poetry, Hollander did it all. As J.D. McClatchy was quoted in his obituary in *The New York Times:* "It is said of a man like John Hollander that when he dies it is like the burning of the library at Alexandria."

In fact, Hollander's career as an esteemed editor and literary scholar and critic has overshadowed his work as a poet. You might be hard pressed these days to find young poets or readers who are excited about Hollander's poetry, beyond the quads of Yale, where he taught for many years —and perhaps understandably so. I for one find the vast majority of Hollander's verse entirely insufferable. His intellectual rigor and range and his playful wit are all quite praiseworthy, but it hasn't always made for the most engaging verse:

> After issues raised first by the dawn
> Had been considered for a while and (darn
> It!) lost their appeal, some agent of the dark
> Stabbed at the afternoon as if with a dirk:
> The disappearance of the sun's red disk
> In a sea of golden dust brought us to dusk.

That's the opening stanza of "Getting From Here to There," from Hollander's 1999 collection *Figurehead and Other Poems*. One can hardly blame a reader for being dissuaded by the combination of Hollander's essayistic tone ("issues raised") with his exhaustive wordplay (dawn/darn, dark/dirk, disk/dust/dusk). The lines flaunt their own artifice and flout the faith we supposedly place in words, showcasing the tottering between meanings that is possible in the slip of just one letter to another. And yet, of lines like these, one could say (and here Hollander seems to be Heaney's exact opposite) that they are interesting, but never that they are important.

The rhetorical ease of late Auden (but not his moral questioning) and the high abstraction of Wallace Stevens (but not his aesthetic questing) are everywhere in Hollander. Consider the final lines of the 169th poem in his long, sonnet-esque sequence *Powers of Thirteen*, from 1983 (each poem is 13 lines; 13 raised to the second power is 169). The speaker and addressee are first compared to light and sound "disputing / Claims for primacy at the morning of the world," then to "object and image,"

> Moving toward the mirror's surface each through the magic
> Space that the other's world must needs transform in order
> To comprehend; when our voices have surrounded one
> Another, each like some penumbra of resonance.
> So that you have the last word now I give it to you.

The lines, though certainly beautiful, would seem to need to outpace their own literary echoes (Stevens, first of all) and archaisms ("must needs") and their own cleverness in order to also be powerful. Hollander won the Bollingen Prize for *Powers of Thirteen;* let it never be said that he was not an extremely accomplished and well-respected poet. Whether he is one who will continue to be read is another question. In *The New York Times Book Review*, the poet Paul Zwieg once called Hollander "a virtuoso without a subject matter," and reading Hollander's work today, this seems quite accurate. Hollander's book-length poem *Reflections on Espionage: The Question of Cupcake*, published in 1974, may be the most egregious example. Just because you *could* write a book-length poem written as pseudo-diary entries of a secret agent codenamed Cupcake is no reason to actually *do* it.

What *should* we read of Hollander's work then? Perhaps we might return to our original question: What did he translate?

————

In Hollander's case there is a very small body of translation, but its impact on his own work is, I would argue, immense. In 1969, at the request of Irving Howe, Hollander translated several poems from Yiddish for anthology titled *A Treasure of Yiddish Poetry*. Although the poems are relatively minor, Hollander later told an interviewer that his engagement with Yiddish poetry had a way of "unlocking" something about his own poetry:

In the course of that work, I discovered the poet Moishe-Leib Halpern, and my translations of him were lucky. More than that, they seemed to help me develop a certain tonal mode in my own poems. That is, what I had to do to translate certain poems of Halpern's, I've now retained as a vocal element.

Yiddish has a relatively short history as a literary language; as most of its poetry has been written since the 19th century, certain aspects are foreshortened: one becomes more aware of the presence of vernacular phrases and colloquialisms, for example. In any case, those poems from the Yiddish were the final translations Hollander completed for many years. But what they unlocked for him may have been essential.

Hollander's most important and best work, in my estimation, is the long poem *Spectral Emanations*, published in 1978. The poem is bizarre, freakishly complex, and funny, and powerful. Subtitled "A Poem in Seven Branches in Lieu of a Lamp," and dedicated to the memory of his father, Hollander's sequence "kindl[es] the light of sound" and recreates a corollary to the golden lamp of the Second Temple in Jerusalem, which was supposedly carried to Rome in the Triumph of Titus, and rumored to have been lost off the Milvian bridge when Constantine converted to Christianity. Hollander's poem is written in seven sections of poetry and prose, which correspond to the seven branches of the menorah, the seven colors of the rainbow, and seven celestial bodies. There are even — a note tells us — factorial seven divided by 10, or 504, lines in the seven sections of 72 lines each. But here, Hollander's virtuosic wit takes on mystic weight — perhaps because the lines, from the first section (Red) and on, sing and lurch with crucial music:

> Now at this red moment
> He forgets his city
> As his tongue is made to
> Fuck the roof of his mouth,
> His skull cradling little
> Ones of brain is dashed now
> Against rock, and the pulp
> Of him slips to the ground.

Vernacular, even vulgar diction ("Fuck the roof") and erratic comma splices are interrupted by powerful enjambments that either skewer axiomatic phrases ("little / Ones") or manufacture archaic-seeming inversions ("Of him slips"). Despite its intricate superstructures, the poem reads like a fugue state, its varying line-lengths shot-through with sections of Old Testament-infused prose (reminiscent of the playful and vaguely Early Modern prose stanzas of Robert Duncan): "At first our heroes stood for us, then among us, when we stood for ourselves; now they do not even represent our sorrows. The Paul Bunyan balloon was deflated and put away when Thanksgiving had passed [...] and the Book of the People of the Book is in tatters." And yet, one realizes, the poem proceeds and recedes in careful concert: The lines are syllabic, starting with six ("Red") and proceeding to eight ("Orange"), 10 ("Yellow"), 12 ("Green"), then down again by twos, back to six ("Violet").

So the poem is highly formal, highly wrought, and yet vulgar, funny, and playful. But nowhere else in Hollander does his playfulness take on such sinister implications. Frequently among the voices and images filtering and flickering through the poem is a register in which the lamp, conflated with poetic insight, is an anonymous weapon. Consider prose segments from the "Blue" section:

> The laser-eye is itself dangerous, for like a speaking, destroying word of light it can nullify your subjects as if they were chaoses, but leave you not alone, merely a hologram of yourself and yet accompanied still.
>
> The control panel is located deep inside, although an unreliable terminal is available at the top, from which there is a synoptic but distorted view of the power units.
>
> [...]
>
> Wait for the blue light to shine.
>
> Remember that they are all despots.
>
> If you get it to work properly, it will put an end to them, your predecessors.

Those lines seem simultaneously to beam themselves in from the realm of science-fiction, like cold instructions for a poetic weapon of mass destruction — and yet, at the same time, to frighteningly and obliquely reference the historical acts of vast destruction perpetrated against Jewish people before and since the sacking of the Second Temple. Whether it was the colloquial tone that Hollander retained from his translations of Yiddish, or simply a willingness to engage with a subject matter that could shade his wit, Hollander has here channeled a vein of poetic waters through a complicated set of sluices such that the refracted fragments of color and language do indeed "kindle the light of sound."

Harold Bloom wrote in a long essay on *Spectral Emanations* that he "[did] not hesitate to proclaim [it] as one of the central achievements of [Hollander's] generation, matching the long poems of Merrill, Ashbery, and Ammons." And I would agree: the poem, with its strictures and pyrotechnics, is, and will be, inspired.

A writer's death can be like a critical sunspot, blinding us to their flaws, or it can bring to light a more rational assessment of the poet's place in the narrative we call a canon. Heaney, for example, certainly merits the outpouring of superlatives that followed his death, but he also represents everything that Language poetry (which has become "the mainstream," if poetry can have a mainstream) has increasingly defined itself *against* for the past 40 years: the sovereign speaker, narrative, the Bard who gives his readings in that unmistakable Poet Voice, formalism. Heaney was out of fashion at the time of his death, but in the wake of his death, we're inclined to think he is timeless. But will he be? Hollander poses an opposite question: he never became the calcified, monolithic "Famous Seamus" that Heaney became, but in his restless formal virtuosity and curiosity he hasn't left audiences with a salient subject matter or a famous work, either.

Considering the poet at the limits of his or her language — considering the poet's *translations* — may be one way to ground our critical assessment not simply in the shifting sands of contemporary reputation or stylistic fads. In the case of Heaney, I believe his *Beowulf* will prove to be an important contribution to the canon of English literature, but also an important "rhyme" between his own poetry and that canon; I believe we will be reading Heaney, both his Old English and his own work, for many, many years. In the case of Hollander, his translations may have "unlocked" the best of his work — *Spectral Emanations* — but whether that work will gain the audience it deserves remains to be seen. ✥

NOW THE GREEN BLADE RISETH

SUSAN STRAIGHT

They were stopped at the long signal light on Jacaranda Avenue. "Can we go by Rite Aid? I need shampoo." She had to use his Head and Shoulders that morning, and it made her hair feel dry as broom bristles. She twisted it into the bun but she hated the smell. She wanted Suave Juicy Green Apple.

"Fuck!" he shouted. "I don't have time for that! Women get in a Rite Aid and they start looking at whatever they look at! Mascara!" He said the word wrong. Mus-ca-ra.

She had closed her eyes. He would bring his hand to the side of her throat for two seconds. He had started that a few weeks ago. Fingers just circling, thumb under her jaw. He would breathe into her ear and say, "I — don't — have — time — for — this." Whatever it was.

The blinker. She could hear the blinker. The metronome. When she was seven, she had two lessons. Her mother wanted her to play piano in a church someday. The teacher was a woman from Crystal Cathedral. Tap/breath tap/breath tap/breath. Two different fingernails on a glass table.

He had turned the radio off. He never turned sports radio off after a game. The endless blustery voices. Free throws. Kobe. Dwight. Waste of talent. Selfish. Lazy. Incredible. She always thought of a word her father said was considered terrible for humans but totally fine for animals — dismemberment. They dismembered the game, every minute of it. He never turned the voices off.

They were in the crosswalk, only a foot from the bumper. And when he blew out of his nostrils very soft it was like a baby bull. Ferdinand the Bull.

The mother pushed a Ralphs cart with three plastic bags in the belly and one jug of water on the shelf. The daughter walked beside the cart like it was a horse on the pioneer trail and not her turn to ride. She had on tight jeans shorts and a black T-shirt too big so it was knotted into a bulb at her back. She was drinking Sierra Mist — green plastic bottle. She skipped ahead two steps in the crosswalk, and then close to the curb she slowed down again and stayed right beside that pony. Her mother said something to her and the girl pushed the button to cross up San Anselmo. Vic was waiting to turn right. Now he'd have to wait for them, too, and that would piss him off if they were slow. With the cart, they'd be slow. ⚏

FACING: MATT SIEGLE, *CAR* (DETAIL), 2013, GRAPHITE ON PAPER, 19" X 15" (FRAMED)

THERE THERE

ALICE BOLIN

I live in Los Angeles. That is, I am in Los Angeles, and I am, ostensibly, alive.

I don't know what else you call it when you come to Los Angeles but then your job prospects fall through and you have to survive on your wits and your friends' couches and your birthday money.

I had never even been to California before this June. As I drove down from the Sierra Nevada foothills on Highway 20 ("The 20"? I'm still working out the local verbal quirks) toward my aunt and uncle's house in the northern Sacramento Valley, I found myself exclaiming out loud to no one, "Look, a palm tree!" Growing up in Idaho, my entire frame of reference for California was as somewhere people retired to the Northwest from, and as a place that was vaguely "fancy." I still have difficulty shaking that last idea. When I discovered I didn't get cell phone service in my aunt and uncle's house, I could only think, outraged, "In *California*?"

My more recent frame of reference for California comes from books, which tend to paint it as a sun-drenched and schizophrenic collection of tropes revolving clumsily around a nonexistent center. Joan Didion has devoted at least a portion of each of her essay collections to trying to understand California; she spends all of her 2003 book *Where I Was From* parsing the state's contradictions.

"This book represents an exploration into my own confusions about the place," she writes early in *Where I Was From*, "… misapprehensions and misunderstandings so much a part of who I became that I can still to this day confront them only obliquely." These misunderstandings are mostly related to the way that California's imagination of itself — as native, independent, wild — is at odds with what has from the beginning been its essential character — as immigrant, corporate, tamed, and developed. As Didion writes in *Where I Was From*, "A good deal about California does not, on its own preferred terms, add up." Or as she quotes from W. B. Yeats in the epigraph to her first essay collection, *Slouching Towards Bethlehem*, "The center cannot hold."

Or as my cousin Tony told me in a dark comedy club in Santa Monica, "There is no there there." This might be Gertrude Stein's most Gertrude Stein-y quote, but it is not that sphinxlike when taken in context. She was describing how she felt when revisiting her childhood home in

Oakland: the loss one can feel for a place when its fundamental character has been so changed that, while it isn't gone, it can no longer be said to be *there* either.

But Stein's koan works just as well when describing the literal and existential decentralization one experiences in Los Angeles. I missed three-quarters of the show that night, including Tony's set, because I couldn't find the comedy club; I wandered dumbfounded around Santa Monica's prefab "promenade," two sterile streets of luxury storefronts and chain restaurants, passing the same stores again and again, until I realized that I had actually been circling around the club — it was tucked in an alley, the entrance to which could be found, I was told later, because it is "near the Hooters."

I was in a poisonous mood when I drove to West Hollywood, bought Raymond Chandler's 1949 novel *The Little Sister* at Book Soup, and went to a Thai restaurant across Sunset to sullenly stare at its cover and eat noodles. In it I found private detective Philip Marlowe at his most bitchy and pessimistic. "I'm just sitting here because I don't have any place to go," he tells a client. "I don't want to work. I don't want anything." When I read that I said silently to Marlowe, "Preach."

A majority of the appeal of Chandler's novels revolves around Marlowe, a jaded and impossibly savvy outsider whose general disdain for women makes him irresistible to them. "What a way you have with the girls," the beautiful movie star Marlowe is working for in *The Little Sister* says to him. "How the hell do you do it, wonderful? With doped cigarettes? It can't be your clothes or your money or your personality. You don't have any. You're not too young, nor too beautiful." How Marlowe does it is certainly a valid question. In the world of Chandler's fiction, the answer mostly lies not with him but with the women: they are craven, sex-obsessed, and ambitious, qualities Marlowe has learned to expect and play to. I find this pattern fascinating — Chandler's novels are so misogynist that they somehow veer away from the offensive, pointing toward a complex in their hero.

Marlowe's ambivalent sexuality always becomes a mechanism of the novels' plots: if he is attracted to a woman — whether she is beautiful or plain, seemingly worldly or innocent — it means she is troubled, hiding dark secrets, and quite probably amoral and dangerous. In *The Little Sister*, he is enlisted by a nerdy and prudish teenager from Manhattan, Kansas, named Orfamay Quest to track down her older bother. Marlowe finds her uptight and irritating, and she can only offer him 20 dollars for his services, but he still takes the case. "I was just plain bored with doing nothing," Marlowe says to explain why he agreed to work for her, but then he adds, "Perhaps it *was* the spring too. And something in her eyes that was much older than Manhattan, Kansas."

Marlowe chases this glimmer of sex in Orfamay's eyes, stealing a kiss from her along the way to discovering that she is involved with blackmailing her sister and murdering her brother. Heterosexual relationships are depicted as dangerous — one must balance the necessity of sex with the impossibility of trust. In fact, one of Marlowe's only positive relationships in all of Chandler's novels is with a man, Terry Lennox, in *The Long Goodbye*. Like his female paramours,

Marlowe finds himself strangely drawn to Lennox, a war hero and alcoholic who has been accused of murdering his wife. Marlowe helps Lennox flee to Mexico and ends up in jail for him; although Marlowe has mixed feelings about the lengths he goes to protect Lennox, he is more purely devoted to him than any of the women he is sexually involved with. At times Marlowe makes me think of Patricia Highsmith's great sociopath hero, Tom Ripley. But the connection between Ripley's sexual problems and the things he is driven to do is spelled out more plainly: it is closeted homosexuality pushed to pathology.

Of course, Chandler is also just participating in one of the noir genre's great tropes: the femme fatale, who appears as seductive and seemingly helpless, when she is in fact self-serving, traitorous, and possibly bloodthirsty. It is a trope that reveals a deep fear of women and sex. Many of these women are described as nymphomaniacs, like the sex-crazed and deranged younger Sternwood daughter in *The Big Sleep*, and, in *The Little Sister*, the sultry, sinister film star Dolores Gonzales. "You always wear black?" Marlowe asks Gonzales. "But yes. It is more exciting when I take my clothes off," she replies. "Do you have to talk like a whore?" he says. "I wear black because I am beautiful and wicked — and lost," Gonzales eventually explains, in one of the more breathtakingly obvious descriptions of the femme fatale in all of literature.

Some femmes fatales knowingly use their sexuality to get ahead. "I do not draw a very sharp line between business and sex," Gonzales says in *The Little Sister*. "Sex is a net with which I catch fools." But others are unconsciously, mysteriously driven to ruin and manipulate men — modern sirens enticing men to rocky shores. This is the case with Faye Greener in Nathanael West's great Los Angeles novel *The Day of the Locust*. She is a shallow and amoral teenage actress who inspires every male character in the novel with a crazy, infuriating desire. "She lay stretched out on the divan with her arms and legs spread, as though welcoming a lover, and her lips were parted in a heavy, sullen smile," West writes, describing a photograph Faye has given the book's protagonist, Tod Hackett. "She was supposed to look inviting, but the invitation wasn't to pleasure."

The Day of the Locust is a deeply, almost hysterically misogynistic book. The men in it are desperate to physically control and punish Faye, purely because of the desire she elicits in them. This male paranoia in West's and Chandler's work seems related to their vision of Los Angeles: as alien territory ruled by no knowable order. The fact that women in Los Angeles could be deceitful, ambitious, and in control confirmed it as a kind of bizarro world — and confirmed that any hero who braved its borders, no matter how many Los Angeles eccentrics surrounded him, would be truly alone.

I was staying in Long Beach with my friend James and his brother John, in their bachelor pad furnished only with two deck chairs, two air mattresses, a 42-inch flat-screen television, and an inflatable raft for a sofa. James and John are both railroad conductors, and they work insane hours: they get called into work in the middle of the night, and every trip they are gone for days at a time. I was sitting around their apartment alone one night when I came across *The Big Lebowski* in a pile of DVDs. I was aware that the movie was iconic and beloved, but I had somehow never seen it, so I put it on the big screen and settled in on the raft. And I loved it! What a good movie!

The movie's slacker hero, The Dude, is drawn into a kidnapping case in which a millionaire with The Dude's same name, Jeff Lebowski, asks him to track down his nymphomaniac (!) wife; as he unravels the mystery, he has encounters with various Hollywood weirdos. The Dude is a league bowler, unemployed, and terminally laid back, but just like Philip Marlowe, trouble finds him. In fact, I was struck by how reminiscent *The Big Lebowski* was of Chandler, an insight that, it turns out, is either pretty perceptive or totally obvious. In the second paragraph of the movie's Wikipedia article, I learned that the Coen brothers had "wanted to do a Chandler kind of story — how it moves episodically, and deals with the characters trying to unravel a mystery, as well as having a hopelessly complex plot that's ultimately unimportant."

The Big Lebowski is an innovative detective story because it is infused with western genre elements, like its mysterious cowboy narrator who waxes folksy at the beginning and end of the film and shows up twice at the bowling alley bar to order a sarsaparilla. The Dude's nickname brilliantly recalls both the cowboys of the Old West and the stoners of the New West. Los Angeles has a strange dual relationship to the cowboy, given that cowboys were a real part of the history of Southern California and California is still a highly agricultural state, but Hollywood also created and propagated the John Wayne–Lone Ranger archetype. It's the mess of reality and fantasy embodied by the buckaroos in *The Day of the Locust*, who live in real cowboy camps in the canyons surrounding Los Angeles but make a living by playing extras in westerns.

It seems the Los Angeles of Chandler, West, and the Coen brothers still retains something of the frontier feeling that has defined the myth of the American West. It is dominated by settlers and transplants, prospectors trying to strike it rich, and the rules can always be rewritten. This is why the hero always finds himself interloping in ever-stranger pockets of the Los Angeles population: Chandler's movie stars, drug dealers, and gangsters; *The Day of the Locust*'s cowboys, midget cock fighters, old vaudeville clowns, and Hollywood madams; and *The Big Lebowski*'s millionaires, conceptual artists, German nihilists, and pornographers. These stories riff on what has always been sold as the American frontier's most attractive and most terrifying quality: anything can happen.

West understood this mandate for reinvention when he said with tongue in cheek that he changed his name from Nathan von Wallenstein Weinstein following Horace Greeley's famous enjoinder, "Go West, young man." But this free-floating potentiality also knocks our Los Angeles heroes — and their creators — perpetually off-balance, keening in astonishment and disgust at what God hath wrought. And their creators, too. West despairs at Los Angeles's manic architectural sensibilities in *The Day of the Locust*: "Only dynamite would be of any use against the Mexican ranch houses, Samoan huts, Mediterranean villas, Egyptian and Japanese temples, Swiss chalets, Tudor cottages, and every possible combination of these styles that lined the slopes of the canyon." Chandler moves beyond West's exhaustion to pure disdain when he talks about "the luxury trades, the pansy decorators, the lesbian dress designers, the riffraff of a big hard-boiled city with no more personality than a paper cup."

As I took the 405 from Long Beach to Carson to Hawthorne to Inglewood to Mar Vista to Culver City to Mid-City and downtown, doubling back on the 101 through Chinatown to Echo Park to Silver Lake to Koreatown to Hollywood to West Hollywood to Beverly Hills,

I was impressed by the unnerving sense of a city that sprang up overnight and sprawled like an invasive species over the landscape. "There ought to be a monument to the man who invented neon lights," Marlowe says in *The Little Sister*. "Fifteen stories high, solid marble. There's a boy who really made something out of nothing." Marlowe's wry hopelessness is reminiscent of the nihilists in *The Big Lebowski*. The archetype isn't called the lonesome cowboy for nothing.

⸺

On Labor Day, James, John, and I celebrated workers' rights by spending the day at Redondo Beach. James wore his Railroad Workers United T-shirt; John wore a shirt he bought at Disneyland with a picture on it of the villain Gaston from Beauty and the Beast looking in a mirror and bold text reading, "Relationship Status? Single."

As my little train conductors frolicked in the surf, I sat on the beach, taking pictures of myself with my phone and letting the sun bake me brick red. The air churned with a weird, hot fog, and kids dragged masses of sea plants from the water and piled them up on the beach. At one point a seagull took a shit on my shirt.

In her 1991 essay "Pacific Distances," Joan Didion writes,

> When I first moved to Los Angeles from New York, in 1964, I found [its] absence of narrative a deprivation. At the end of two years I realized (quite suddenly, alone one morning in the car) that I had come to find narrative sentimental.

Resistance to narrative is a symptom of the city's disjointedness, its failure to cohere, its lack of a meaningful focal point or thesis. This is what sends Marlowe, The Dude, and Tod Hackett spinning from one corner of the city to another, alone and driftless. And this is why the detective story, which of all genres provides the audience with a concrete resolution, when set in Los Angeles feels ironic, anathema — the plot is "ultimately unimportant."

Watching the swimmers at Redondo Beach, I found the ocean played a trick of perspective — the hugeness of the water flattened horizontal distances, so everything, the beach and the surf and the tiny swimmers, hung vertically in the sky. The ocean also runs contrary to our desire for something comprehensive, for a solution. It is a network progressing mysteriously without a discernable center. It's massive and it's moving.

Watching the Pacific that day I felt a scary kind of vertigo, unable to make sense of the distances, unable to stay still in the face of so much motion. Then I saw James rising out of the water; diving in and out of the ocean had burned a raw patch on his stomach. With him as my focus, I leaned in and watched the ocean pull away as he folded toward me, heading in. ⫽

FACING: DAVID SNYDER, *BORDER*, 2013

THE CHRONICLES OF THE VEIL

LAILA LALAMI

Whenever I return to Morocco, I try to visit a bookshop. Among the many pleasures of Moroccan bookshops is the fact that they retain much of their individual character. Some are housed in old, spacious buildings that still have original zellij tile work or wrought-iron windows. Others are more modest, narrow stalls tucked away between a café and another café. A great many of them sell used books or allow you to trade one used book for another. And all of them, all of them, are redolent with the smell of books.

On this particular trip, I happened to be in Rabat on a rainy week in February. The wind rustled the leaves of the palm trees. Along the colonnaded streets of downtown, buses, cars, and motorcycles drove past at frightening speed, leaving behind wet tracks on the asphalt. At nearly every red light, drivers honked at other drivers. But I found refuge from the noise at Kalila wa Dimna Bookshop, where it was warm and quiet.

I was not looking for a specific book that day, but I happened to find a display table piled with recent works by, and about, Moroccan women: not just novels and memoirs by writers like Leila Abouzeid, Fatema Mernissi, Zakya Daoud, and Bahaa Trabelsi, but also a large selection of nonfiction books — so many, in fact, that it was difficult to pick just one or two. There were, for instance, *Atlassiyat*, a collection of interviews with women dissidents of the 1960s; *Printemps et Automne Sexuels*, a study of social attitudes toward puberty and menopause; *Al-onf al-jinsi jarimah*, an anthology of essays on sexual harassment; *La Poterie Marocaine*, a book on women potters from the Rif region; *Une Femme Nommée Rachid*, a memoir by a political activist who spent five years in King Hassan's jails; *Femme Idéale*, a look at the representations of the ideal woman in contemporary Moroccan literature; and many others whose titles I did not jot down in my notebook. In the end, I bought a memoir by Nadia Yassine, an intriguing political figure about whom I wanted to learn more.

How different this book-buying experience was from any visit to a chain bookstore in Los Angeles, where I live now. At my local Barnes & Noble, I usually find, somewhere between the latest diet book and the newest political pamphlet, veil books. You must have seen them, too. On the cover is a woman shrouded in black, her soulful eyes averted from the photographer's gaze.

The title, set in curly Arabesque letters, contains words like *veil*, *honor*, *silence*, and *harem*. I can never remember specific titles, perhaps because they all sound like permutations of one another: *Behind the Veil*, *Lifting the Veil*, *The Veil of Honor*, *The Veil of Silence*, *The Harem of Silence*, *The Silence of the Harem*. As for the story itself, the setting may range from Kabul to Kandahar, but its details rarely change. A feisty young woman, known only by her first name, suffers under the tyrannical rule of her father or her brother or her husband. Then some horrific event — a sexual mutilation, a potential honor killing, a forced marriage — causes her to flee from the father or brother or husband. Often, a concerned Westerner, perhaps a reporter on assignment abroad or a teacher posted at a nearby American school, helps this young woman write her dramatic story of escape, in the hope that it will "raise awareness" about the plight of Muslim women. A few names and identifying details are changed to protect the innocent, and the usual politically correct disclaimers are made about how the practices described run afoul of "true Islam."

The first time I noticed these books — I call them Chronicles of the Veil™ — was about 20 years ago, when I came to California for college. I was desperate to read something besides the linguistics textbooks I was assigned, so on a night out with friends, I stopped by a bookstore in Santa Monica. On a display shelf I noticed Jean Sasson's *Princess: A True Story of Life Behind the Veil in Saudi Arabia*. The titular princess ("Sultana") is a plucky girl, born into a fabulously wealthy household, but where she has no rights and is treated as chattel. Sultana's sister Sara is forced to marry a man in his 60s; her brother Ali is violent toward any women, servants, or animals that cross his path; her mother dies of an inoperable tumor and is buried in an unmarked grave in the desert; immediately afterward, her father marries an underage girl; her friend Nadia is drowned in the family pool as punishment for approaching a man on the street; her Filipino maid's best friend is raped by her employer.

Princess is a surrogate memoir, by which I mean that Sasson writes in the first person, taking on the voice of Sultana. But, even though the book is billed as a true story, the life it describes is rich in convenient coincidences. Each of Sultana's friends, family members, or acquaintances seems to personify a specific, totemic fault within Saudi society — underage marriage, violence against women, abuse of foreign workers. The prose is peppered with asides about the unrelenting oppression of women and the equally unrelenting brutality of men, not just in Saudi Arabia, but in the entire Middle East. "[The girls] might meet a nice foreign man and marry him. Any man was better than a Saudi man!" "It is never the fault of the man in the Middle East. Even if he murders his wife, the man will state 'valid' reasons for his action, which will be accepted by other men without question." "No one will ever admit to the death of a loved one. The furthest an Arab will go in delivering bad news is to prepare the family for worse news from the doctor."

I remember I was horrified when I read *Princess* because it contained so much violence against women, so much brutality on every page. But I was also troubled by the complete absence of dissenting voices. My experience of the world was that wherever there is oppression, there is resistance, too, yet the book made it seem as if all the women in Saudi Arabia — all except the pseudonymous Sultana, speaking through the voice of Jean Sasson — had resigned themselves to their plight and had no hope of a better future. The implication, of course, was that Saudi women had to be saved.

I was struck then, and I suppose I still am now, by how different the Chronicles of the Veil™ were from the books I had read when I was growing up. Those books were written by

Moroccan women and for Moroccan women; the authors explicitly critiqued the laws, cultural customs, and religious beliefs that hampered Moroccan women and prevented them from achieving full equality. But the books I encountered in America, particularly in commercial bookstores, were general, even generic, in their approach. They were often set in Afghanistan, Pakistan, or Saudi Arabia. They spoke breathlessly about "Muslim women," a population so large and so diverse that hardly any statements made about them bear scrutiny. What could possibly be said to be true of 800 million women, spread out over 56 countries, dozens of ethnic groups, and a multitude of legal and cultural practices?

There came a moment when I realized that there are two distinct kinds of conversations taking place around Muslim women — one in Muslim countries and one in Western countries. The first conversation is highly specific, and focuses on local problems. In Morocco, for example, feminist activists pushed for a reform of family law for more than a decade; it was finally passed by parliament in 2004, and it granted women greater rights in marriage, divorce, and custody. Now these activists are pushing for another reform, this time of the penal code, because it contains a loophole that allows a man to escape statutory rape charges in case of marriage. Feminists are also focusing on access to education in rural areas, the practice of hiring underage girls as domestic workers, sexual harassment on the street — these are issues that Moroccan women and girls face every day, but they might not be exactly the same issues faced by women in Somalia or Comoros, where the legal apparatus and cultural practices are quite different.

The second kind of conversation takes place in Western countries, primarily via the Chronicles of the Veil™ and other sensationalistic materials. Here, the terms of the debate are global. One hears about arranged marriages, forced veiling, honor killings, female genital mutilations, and punishment by stoning, the narrative line always the same: Muslim women are victims, and they need Western saviors. So simple and so powerful is this message that even when Muslim women speak out against it, their supposed saviors refuse to believe them. Last April, for instance, when the Ukrainian group FEMEN staged topless protests outside mosques in Europe, billing them as "International Topless Jihad Day," Muslim women organized their own counterprotests online, in which they made clear they did not need FEMEN's help. But FEMEN's Inna Shevchenko's response was, "through all history of humanity, all slaves deny that they are slaves. [...] [These Muslim women] write on their posters that they don't need liberation, but in their eyes it's written *help me*."

What happens once Western readers have had their "awareness raised" about the plight of Muslim women? Are they able to identify the legal, educational, economic, or religious mechanisms that create this oppression? Can they point to the role their own governments sometimes play in perpetuating these mechanisms? Do they become allies of the numerous local organizations that work on the ground to bring about change? Not really. Instead, they feel "concern" about these women, feel that these women need to be "saved" somehow, and probably also feel relief that they are not among them. In the end, the Chronicles of the Veil™ create a debate *about* Muslim women, not *with* them. This is a debate that serves to console, rather than inform. It provides even the most conservative of Americans the opportunity to present themselves as defenders of Muslim women's rights. (Rick Santorum, for example, is against contraception for American women, but is apparently also a "steadfast ally" of Muslim women and girls.)

Not long ago, at a dinner party in Los Angeles, I happened to mention these two distinct conversations about Muslim women, only to be met with befuddlement. To my guest, a middle-aged academic, it seemed ungrateful that I should refuse the attention of people who are so intent on my liberation. For me, any fruitful conversation about Muslim women must begin by rejecting the simplistic category "Muslim women," a category that often results in a denial of these women's multifarious agency. There are thousands and thousands of Muslim activists, men and women alike, working for gender equality in the Muslim world, sometimes at great risk to themselves. Bringing them into the debate — talking to them, not about some abject "representative" — is the only way to advance it. ⌗

SAY THEY'RE PRETTY:
On Fictional Characters and Real Life

JOHN RECHY

From where do a writer's characters come? Who are they, finally? — these wily, shifty creatures, darting in and out of trouble, creatures who cajole, flirt with their author, seduce him, at times challenge him to the point that they run away beyond their creator's intent. Don Quixote fought his most formidable battle not with windmills but with Cervantes, who detested him, ridiculed him, tortured him. And who won in that epic battle between the author and his character? Don Quixote — by evolving into myth, becoming a figure of pathos, a noble hero in search of the impossible dream; and he is that even for those who do not know who Cervantes is. Still, it was Cervantes who imbued him with the characteristics that allowed his character to triumph.

Many characters, of course, come from real life, even though at times they sidle into one's stories unrecognized until they threaten to sue one.

Christopher Isherwood gave me what I thought was sage advice on using real people in one's writing. He told me, "You can question their morals, call them liars, expose them as thieves — as long as you describe them as attractive."

Several instances in my life have tested that admonition. In my first novel, *City of Night*, I described a male nurse I knew as a deceiver, entirely unethical, prone to collect credit cards from his dead patients. I received an angry letter from him in which he asked: "Do I really strike you as being coldly blond?"

In a short story that would become a part of that same novel, I wrote about a downtown Los Angeles queen who called herself Miss Destiny and dreamt of one day having a white wedding. Titled "The Fabulous Wedding of Miss Destiny," that story appeared in a small literary journal called *Big Table*. I thought no one would read it. As I strolled one afternoon along Hollywood Boulevard, I heard a voice calling: "John Rechy! John Rechy!"

For the longest time, I preferred to be anonymous, like others in the world of the streets I was living within, a world hidden to all but those who existed in it. So I was startled to hear my name called. There, jaywalking toward me, impervious to protesting honks, came Miss Destiny. "My dear!" she trilled, "I want to thank you for making me even more famous!"

At times one has to veer away from reality in order to bring fiction to life. I had augmented the real Miss Destiny's effervescent stories to give them resonance, and, I hoped, more wistful poetry. Subsequently, she absorbed the characteristics of my character; she told her stories with my embellishments, claimed they were her exact words. She landed on the cover of *ONE Magazine*, in full wedding drag, demurely, as "The Fabulous Miss Destiny," and she gave a nasty untrue interview about me, but I forgave her because she described me as "cute." (For years afterwards, she would call me, always very late at night and in a boozy voice ask me to please inform whomever she was with that she was indeed "the fabulous Miss Destiny" of my novel. Of course I obliged. A few years ago the calls stopped; and I hope — assume — Miss Destiny has kept her intention to "storm heaven and protest.")

I once — and quite literally — became a character from one of my own books. My second novel, *Numbers*, was set mainly in Griffith Park, its protagonist a young man named Johnny Rio, who spends his idle time seeking adventures in the park. I was idling in the same park one afternoon — still anonymous — when a stranger braked his car to tell me that someone had written a book about me. "Who?" I asked, befuddled. "His name is John Rechy," he said, "but I don't think that's his real name because nobody would write a book like that under his own name." As he left, he called back, "Goodbye, Johnny Rio."

The sternest test of Isherwood's admonition about permission to describe real persons even as morally decadent as long as they're described as attractive occurred when I modeled a character after him. Without using his actual name, I described him in my novel *Numbers* as somewhat randy in his cups — pardon the appropriately dated euphemism; but I had also described him as an attractive middle-aged man, to the point that the painter Cadmus, recognizing him, said I had been too kind. The purveyor of the advice I had followed was outraged. An invitation made earlier to dinner at his home was withdrawn with an angry telegram from his longtime companion on behalf of them both; the enraged companion proposed a near-duel — I mean it — a strict confrontation — although I had described him as being "pretty."

One might be tempted to claim that some characters are divinely inspired. I was sunbathing one summer day when, looking up, I saw two long clouds sailing toward each other to form a cross. What, I wondered, would some of the Mexican Catholic women I had known in El Paso when we lived in the government projects make of that? I rushed home to write a short story about such a woman, who interprets the configuration as the first portent of a possible miracle, all that can save her at a time of crisis. Inspired, I finished a rough draft in a few hours. When my partner, Michael, came home, I read him the story. "You've got to write a whole novel about her," he exhorted me.

I started *The Miraculous Day of Amalia Gómez*. Soon I encountered a problem. The woman's antecedents were many, and I was creating a unique one. I did not want to risk her becoming a figure in an allegory.

I marvel at the fact that destiny exists only in retrospect, when a series of coincidences string together into inevitability. On such a fateful day, I had gone to a Thrifty Drug Store to buy a beach chair — and I hope you don't think I spend all my time lounging under the sun. The store was out of those chairs. A clerk recommended another store. I drove out of my way to that other store. I should have heard destiny spinning. I walked in, and halted in awe of one of the most gorgeous creations I have ever seen.

She was a Mexican-American woman, not yet 40. She had luscious black hair, waves and waves of it — and into those luminous cascades she had placed a fresh rose, red against the black of her hair. She was a few pounds heavier than she might claim to be — the word "lush" occurred to me. She was dressed in a fashion beyond fashion, entirely her own. In a gesture of decorum, she had added to her red blouse a lacy ruffle that, however, did not compromise the splendid fullness of her breasts. It occurred to me, then, that, rather than having tried for decorum, she had actually called more attention to her ample endowment with the enamored ruffle. She wore a dark skirt with winking slits on either side of her legs and over sling pumps.

There was my flesh-and-blood Amalia!

I followed her along the aisles. Noticing me, she added to her stride a slight swing of her hips. I pursued her, until, at another aisle, a Mexican man with an aggressive mustache — he was shorter than me, I'm delighted to tell you—stood in my path. "Pos?" he challenged me. "Well, nothing," I answered. The woman looked somewhat thrilled, as if she might welcome a good fight over her. And yet — and this in retrospect was what had held me spellbound — there was something yearning, something touchingly defiant about her bold presentation. It was to her that I would donate the enigma of the intersecting clouds.

No other character of mine has taken over her life as did Amalia. Because I came to love her — and imbued her with much of my beloved sister Olga's sauciness — I winced when she refused to heed danger signals. A woman on the brink of disastrous revelations, she continued to court even more disaster. Stop, Amalia! I wanted to scream. She plunged ahead stubbornly, determined finally to triumph, or surrender in defeat. I left it up to her.

I discover this over and over about fictive characters: For them to live fully, one must allow them to be true to themselves, the traits, the characteristics, the contradictions, the background one gives them. One mustn't interfere once that creation springs to life. I tell my writing students: pursue your characters relentlessly, corner them, don't let them get away with anything. I add: In life, be kind. In your art, be ruthless.

There are times when one has to change real-life protagonists into exaggerations to see them clearly, create a close-up of their souls. I spent a summer once as the guest of a fascinating man on his private island. I spent a summer once as the guest of a fascinating man on his private island, along with a cast of exotic guests, one of whom threatened to drown me in the lake. In my novel, I converted them all into vampires, and titled the book that; a motley crew, decadent, degenerate, evil — and gorgeous.

On Venice Beach one afternoon along the boardwalk, a youngish man in jockey shorts and cowboy boots was performing there, dancing and singing and playing a guitar. Nearby a pretty girl with him looked at him sadly while passersby giggled and nudged each other and heckled the man, even while dropping money in his hat. What had led him there?

I subsequently found out that the same man went on to become notorious as the Naked Cowboy — a silly figure courting derision, dancing almost naked on Times Square even in snowy winter.

I didn't like the actual life revealed of the man who had moved me on the beach. So I gave him another life. In my next novel, *The Life and Adventures of Lyle Clemens*, I took him from the beach and left him in front of the Egyptian Theater, attempting to add grandeur to his performance. There, he still sings and dances in boots and jockeys but now to expiate a painful humiliation in his dead mother's life. I was able to stop the heckling and derision by having him plaintively sing his mother's favorite song, "Amazing Grace" — and I released waves of radiant sunshine sweeping along Hollywood Boulevard. That is one of the beauties of the artistic creation, to, in a way, save real-life characters from a shoddy life, to allow them redemption.

There are those who might consider less noble some reasons for casting real people as characters. When a critic has been personally and gratuitously nasty about me while ostensibly reviewing one of my books — and there have been those — she or he is reserved a place in every novel I write, assigned a minor but revealing role — say, as a mudwrestling entrepreneur, or a babbling rhyming weatherman. *In The Life and Adventures of Lyle Clemens*, I extended that to make a political statement, using the names, slightly altered, of malicious Supreme Court justices; "Thomas Clarence" became a small-loans bank clerk; "Antonin Scala" an exploiter of young star map sellers. Discretion cautions me to tell you what Sandra Mae O'Connell did on the set of the pornographic movies produced by the company owned by Mr. and Mrs. Rehnquist.

I justify this practice by pointing out that I am in the tradition of Alexander Pope, Jonathan Swift, Samuel Butler, Anthony Burgess, Walt Whitman.

In a recent novel, *The Coming of the Night*, I included a character loosely modeled after a famous male porn performer whose family cruelly disowned him. After he died, the opportunistic family sued the producers of his movies, my publisher, Grove Press, and myself for — of all things — besmirching the notorious man's reputation. I had not even known him, did not use his real name, wrote sympathetically about him, and I even disguised him by changing a famous tattoo of a kangaroo on his left buttock to that of a rabbit on his right one.

At times real people turn themselves into fictive characters. Along Melrose Avenue once, a man sprinted toward me, his hands imitating a shotgun aimed at me — "Bang, bang, bang! Don't you recognize me?" I remembered him, vaguely, from some brief encounter. "I'm Orin, in your book, the ending, remember? Bang, bang." He was referring to a character in my book *Bodies and Souls*, its ending. "You described me exactly. Blue eyes, ashy blond hair, mysterious — and great looking. I'll be terrific in the movie version, I'll drop by my photo and resume."

Not all such street encounters are that benign. One late night on a darkened street, a bear of a man, who seemed created by the foggy night itself, came at me shouting his anger at my nonfiction book *The Sexual Outlaw*, with its dozens of real people rendered anonymously, among whom I gathered he had seen himself. I made the mistake of turning away from the enraged man, only to feel his huge fist pound the back of my head. As I fell, I heard him bellowing my name interspersed with loud curses. When I managed to get up, a flighty young man who had seen the encounter while cruising the area said to me, "Listen, you can't please everyone."

At the Wax Museum in Buena Park, I stood before the waxy replication of an idol of mine, Marilyn Monroe, herself a sublime work of art. There, watching in awe, was a pretty teenage girl eating an ice cream cone; with her were two incongruous young men, a lanky cowboy-type and a young man dressed in somber black. A fatally cheerful older woman sidled up with her tiny silent husband and said to the girl, "Well, you look like Marilyn enough like to be her daughter. They do say she had a daughter. Now what are you three doing in this sinful city that is going to be destroyed in a monstrous earthquake as soon as we leave?" The girl shrugged, baffled. (An aside: That terrible woman recurs in several of my books, a banal messenger of doom, a simple-minded Cassandra.)

Out of that brief encounter I wrote *Marilyn's Daughter*, in which the girl became Normalyn, who travels from Texas to Hollywood to find out whether she is the daughter of the great star and Robert Kennedy. The same wistful girl with the ice cream cone became also one of the main characters in *Bodies in Souls*. Her apparent innocence and confusion about why she was here, and her out-of-place companions, fascinated me to the point that I created a whole novel about them. As they wander seemingly without direction about the city, they encounter a whole range of characters, all based on real people I had intended to write about--including the televangelist Katherine Kuhlman, a Chicano kid from El Paso who had a tattoo of a naked Christ on his back, the extravagantly beautiful porn star I had seen shunned meanly by everyone at the exclusive restaurant Ma Maison.

At times one may become too involved with one's own characters, and they become uncomfortably real.

Bodies and Souls ends with an apocalyptic catastrophe on the freeway, where the lives of all the main characters — twelve of them — disastrously intersect. Who among them would die, who be hurt, who survive? I couldn't bear to decide. So I wrote their names on pieces of paper, and blindly assigned a few to each fate, not checking until I had reached the end of the book. I was appalled by the result. A favorite character died, a hateful one lived. I tried to cheat. But finally I left their fates intact, allowing for the indifferent perfection of accident.

Parents feel sadness when their children grow up and leave, going off into an undefined future. I have felt something like that in letting my characters go, beyond my control, a book ended. Now the doubts: would they be able to fare alone after the last page is finished?

For me, concern grows when I model a character closely on an actual person. If at the end of a book a character is on the brink of giving up or surviving, what choice — if there even was a choice — was made in real life by its antecedent?

Virtually every character in my first novel was modeled after someone I knew, interacted with, sometimes intimately, other times only fleetingly in telling moments. When that novel was published, with all those lives interpreted — or misinterpreted — I was ambushed by guilt. Since many of the characters I had written about were people in a turbulent world then secret except to them, I wondered whether I had betrayed their lives by having lived among them, with them, as one of them, and then violently separating from them, becoming a writer — escaping, as it were — a life that I had recorded having for most no exit.

What, I wondered, happened to Chuck, the lazy cowboy who lingered under apathetic palm trees and the Los Angeles sun in the old Pershing Square? He was genial, popular, a cowboy without a horse — no frontier left to discover — living from day to day as long as his youth survived. In my novel he will always be basking in the warm sun, untroubled, certain that tonight will allow him another tomorrow. In real life, did it? How old would he be now? Alive? The world I shared with him and others was only blocks away from skid row, waiting. Today, whenever I see a derelict of a certain age and bearing the etchings of good looks, I wonder sadly, Is that Chuck?

And what of the real Sylvia? — a mysterious woman seeking her exiled son in gay bars throughout the country. In my fiction, I left her longing still to find him, a possibility. In real life, did she find him? Did she give up the search; did she drown hope in alcohol?

I had written about a young man who had been an object of desire in the Hollywood of the 1950s; I left him on the brink of aging and accepting redemptive self-knowledge. Years later, when I was hitchhiking, still anonymous, an old, sad man, drunk, stopped to give me a ride — and I recognized my once-beautiful character Lance O'Hara.

Finally, there is, unassailably, this to justify it all: within the artistic creation occurs the only means of stopping time. All characters can be brought back to life, simply by opening the first page of a book. Don Quixote begins his quest, the Governess moves undaunted into Bly, Molly pursues the evasive Yes of her ruminations, Marcel struggles for his mother's kiss, Tristram delays his birth, Odysseus is on his way back to Penelope, Emma prepares for the ball, Catherine's ghost searches along the moors, Jose Arcadio Buendia faces the firing squad for a hundred years of solitude.

In a favorite movie of mine, *Moulin Rouge*, the original one by John Huston, about Toulouse-Lautrec, as the artist lies dying, the ghosts of those he has drawn appear as they were when he first saw them — some dancing, others sashaying about, all vibrantly alive again. Zsa Zsa Gabor, playing Jane Averil beautifully, leans over the dying form of the artist who made her immortal and she gushes, "Toulouse, Toulouse, we heard you were dying and we just had to say goodbye."

What a beautiful farewell to a writer that would be. ✍

AMANDA ROSS-HO, *VERTICAL DROPCLOTH QUILT (JACK IN THE PULPIT)*, 2012
CANVAS DROPCLOTH, ACRYLIC PAINT, THREAD
SEWN BY GINA ROSS, 70"X53", COURTESY OF THE ARTIST AND THE APPROACH, LONDON
PHOTO: FXP PHOTOGRAPHY, LONDON

. . . *TWO DEVILS* CONTINUED FROM PAGE 20 . . .

PART III
The Second Devil: René Belbenoit

"The mechanism that directs government cannot be virtuous, because it is impossible to thwart every crime, to protect oneself from every criminal without being criminal too; [...] crime is one of the vital mainsprings of government..."
— Marquis de Sade, *Juliette*

Charles De Rudio's life could have been the plot for a Dumas novel; René Belbenoit's life not only made it into several books, it was made into two films. To paraphrase Mallarmé, everything exists to end up in a movie.

Belbenoit's plucky, gritty past in the Parisian underworld, his heroism during the First World War, and his maladroit theft resulting in his Devil's Island prison sentence were perfect subjects for film — indeed, the first film based on his life was made while he was still in prison, six years before his successful escape. Starring Ronald Colman, *Condemned* was released in 1929 and was based on a novelized version of Belbenoit's life by Blair Niles, an American travel writer and novelist. But because Belbenoit defied all odds and became the most celebrated escapee of Devil's Island, his life had a second act, and a second movie: *Passage to Marseille* (1944), starring Humphrey Bogart — not only was it based on Belbenoit's harrowing escape, but he was also a technical advisor on the film. Belbenoit made the improbable journey from Devil's Island to Tinseltown, and the one from anonymity to fame: he also became a celebrated author when *Dry Guillotine*, his memoir of his 15-year struggle with the French penal system, was published in 1938. Not only did it become a bestseller, it also proved to be the catalyst for change that resulted in the closing of Devil's Island.

René Belbenoit was born in 1899 in Paris. His father was a career conductor in the French railroad system, but his mother, perhaps feeling constrained by the monotony of railroad tracks, abandoned her husband and son just three months after René's birth to become a tutor for the Russian imperial family. Since his father was usually away, Belbenoit was sent to live with his grandparents, who both died when he was 12. The young Belbenoit then moved in with an uncle who was the manager of a Parisian nightclub in Montmartre on the Place Pigalle, the Café du Rat Mort (the Dead Rat). The Rat Mort was notorious, a meeting place of the *haute* and *demi monde*, where artists such as Toulouse-Lautrec had gathered, and where later, The Prince of Wales would go to see Josephine Baker. It was also where petty criminals sought out unsuspecting patrons flush with cash and jewelry, and gamblers gathered to place substantial bets. Belbenoit spent his days earning large tips as a messenger delivering the love letters written by the club's patrons and doing the various tasks they requested, including delivering large sums of money to the gamblers' bookmakers.

On one such occasion, Belbenoit was entrusted with a larger than usual sum that was being bet on a dark horse—it was a 20-to-one long shot. Figuring that the gamblers would lose their money, Belbenoit kept the 2,200 francs (about $11,000). The horse won. Unsure of what to do, the young man came clean to his uncle, promising to use his own money to repay the debt over time. His uncle, enraged at this affront to his family's honor, began to beat him, and Belbenoit fled. Luckily for Belbenoit, it was August 3, 1914, and Germany had just declared war on France. Paris was filled with anxiety and excitement, and the stolen money suddenly receded into the background as preparations for war became paramount. Belbenoit joined the thousands of young men who were enlisting in the army. His age was overlooked by eager recruiters, and he became a diligent soldier, rising to the rank of corporal. After the Armistice he served as a sergeant in Syria but became ill with a fever in 1920. Sent back to France along with 14 other sick soldiers, he was one of only five to survive the outbreak. Shades of De Rudio.

Belbenoit was recuperating in a hospital near Paris when he met a young nurse, serendipitously named Renée. They fell in love and planned to get married. Belbenoit was honorably discharged in 1921 and set about to find work so that he could support his future bride. Unable to find a job in Paris and completely broke, he headed southeast to Besançon where he heard a dishwashing job was available. He was hired, but after 11 days, he realized that his meager salary would barely support him, let alone a wife. Spying a wallet with 4,000 francs in the kitchen where he worked, Belbenoit lifted it and fled to Paris. Outfitted with smart new clothes that he thought would impress his fiancée and with cash in his pocket, he suddenly began to feel better about his future. But after three days, guilt plagued the young veteran. He wrote a note to Renée saying he had to leave town and boarded a train for Nantes, where he thought he would be less noticeable. His hunch was correct, and he immediately found work as a valet for a countess. (A few aristocratic families managed to avoid losing their heads during the Revolution, and subsequent laws permitted them to retain their titles.)

After a month working in the countess' chateau, Belbenoit noticed the red leather case containing the countess' pearls along with a packet of cash on her dressing table. Not wishing to be a mere servant any longer, he stole those items and beat it back to Paris. He was arrested immediately. Convicted of theft, he was sentenced to eight years of hard labor on Devil's Island. The law of *doublage* was still in effect, so even if he survived his eight-year sentence, he would be required to spend the rest of his life in French Guiana — a living death sentence.

Since the French penal system in French Guiana had no interest in rehabilitating its deportees, prisoners were prohibited from basic necessities — they were not allowed books, writing material, or access to clergy. It was all punishment, all the time. Violating the law was, in essence, a crime against reason, which came with vicious, state-sanctioned repercussions.

The punishment rarely fit the crime. The French took their laws seriously, and lawbreakers, at least those without connections or access to a good lawyer, were swiftly removed from society, often banished to an overseas hell where there was no chance of redemption. By removing their "undesirables" and exiling them to a virtual underworld, the French pursued a form of eugenics — they wanted to wipe out the criminal element. Any crime could condemn one to a lifetime of torture.

After a grueling transatlantic voyage during which he was locked in a cage (as were all convicts), Belbenoit arrived in French Guiana on June 23, 1923. He was assigned his prison identification number — 46,635 — meaning he was the forty-six thousandth, six hundred and thirty-fifth *condamné* to enter the penal colony since 1852.

Because he had served honorably in the war, Belbenoit was at first entitled to receive lighter work assignments than non-veterans — he was sent to a jungle timber camp where he made the straw hats that convicts wore. Most of the rest of the men in his barracks were assigned to clear timber, a miserable fate. Felling hardwood trees with only a hand axe was extremely physically demanding, especially since all prisoners had to exist on starvation rations: half a pint of coffee in the morning; at noon, 26 ounces of bread, a pint of broth (mostly water) and three ounces of beef (most of which was rotten); and in the evening, two ounces of rice. When there was no rice, dry beans or peas were substituted.

Belbenoit plaited straw all morning, after which he was free to wander through the surrounding jungle. During such excursions, he planned his first escape. (The jailers knew that escape via the jungle was virtually impossible and didn't worry too much about it.) With another prisoner, Belbenoit secretly made a bamboo raft and during an August afternoon, they slid their raft into a tributary of the Maroni River. He wrote in *Dry Guillotine*, "The immensity of the jungle, the deep solitude, our uneasiness because we were running away, all these things melted together into one long nightmare and filled us with dread." They were heading for Dutch Guiana, across the river, but the river was wide with strong currents, and they were inexperienced. After a frustrating night spent attempting to reach the Dutch shore, they finally succeeded. A group of Indians spotted the ragged men immediately and took the hapless escapees to a nearby settlement, where they were put in prison. The next day a launch ferried them back to the French side where they were imprisoned at Saint Laurent, the main prison of the colony. Their escape had lasted 39 hours.

Belbenoit discovered that the 40 other men in his blockhouse had made similar attempts at escaping. Locked in cramped quarters and with their legs in irons at night, prisoners had no chance of escaping this stone barracks. The only windows were small, heavily barred openings in the walls 12 feet above the floor. Fetid air, unsanitary conditions (a bucket served as a toilet), bloodthirsty mosquitoes, and brutal guards created hellish conditions for the prisoners as they awaited a "trial" for the crime of escaping. Once tried, the escapees were usually sentenced to solitary confinement on St. Joseph Island for periods ranging from six months to five years. After three attempts, prisoners were reclassified as "incorrigible" and hence, subject to worse treatment. First escape attempts were not punished as harshly as succeeding ones; after waiting for months in this cesspool, Belbenoit was sentenced to 60 days in the blockhouse after which he was sent back to the jungle work camp. He resolved to escape again — this time, by sea.

Back at the camp, Belbenoit soon became ill from the effects of chiggers, the mites that attach to one's skin, causing intense irritation. If untreated, the rashes become infected, and because his feet were so badly infected, he could no longer stand up. He was sent to the infirmary. After recovering, he was reassigned to the jungle camp, where after just one day, he was bitten by thousands of black ants. Swollen and feverish, Belbenoit returned to the infirmary, where the doctor refused to treat him. He went back to the infirmary every morning for two weeks, and was refused each time. Prison officials were dubious of malingerers, and ultimately, he was punished for trying to evade work — 180 more days in the blockhouse. After completing just over half of this sentence, Belbenoit was pardoned for the remainder — it was Bastille Day and reductions in punishments were occasionally handed out as part of the national festival celebrating liberty, brotherhood, and equality. He also received a new, less harsh work assignment. He became an attendant at the infirmary.

This proved to be a lucky break, for among his tasks was fetching water from a well for the sick inmates. Walking by an orange tree on his way to get the water, Belbenoit filled his buckets not with water but with oranges, which he later sold to inmates for two sous each. Belbenoit, who never lost his street smarts, was able to earn enough money to buy new clothes — his own had turned to rags, and the prison rarely provided new clothes to inmates. Unluckily, a guard soon caught him by the orange tree and demanded the oranges. All kinds of little scams and graft were rampant throughout the colony, as would be expected in such a harsh system. The guard took over the orange business — but told Belbenoit he could gather chestnuts instead. Selling those delicacies, he began to make enough money to buy those things essential to prisoners: tobacco and rum. After a while, he had saved enough to think of another escape. Bribes would be necessary, as would illicitly obtained provisions. Only prisoners with money could hope to escape.

Belbenoit and a group of eight others planned to flee on Christmas Eve, when the guards would be drunk from their holiday rum. The prisoners had hidden a large canoe in the jungle, prepared a water barrel, and packed food rations. They made good on their plan and managed to sail down the Maroni River to its mouth at the Atlantic Ocean. They put out to sea and headed west for Venezuela; that country did not always extradite convicts.

Huge waves began to overtake the canoe, the mast was ripped away, the canoe was taking on water, and the man who had claimed to be an experienced navigator had lied: he had no marine skills whatsoever. What was left of their food was ruined, and the men were forced to head for shore in circumstances that echoed those of De Rudio 65 years earlier. They would have to continue on foot. Because he had jeopardized the entire escape by lying, the false navigator was told to leave and fend for himself. He walked off into the jungle — but returned the next morning, whereupon the largest and strongest of the men killed him. His body was thrown into the ocean. Such was the punishment for one who had risked the lives of his comrades.

The men marched all day in flooded mangrove marshes, smearing mud on their bodies in an attempt to ward off the ravenous mosquitoes. After several days, exhausted, they realized they were lost and could not continue. They had very little food and no possibility of obtaining any. Knowing that they were still close to French Guiana, they decided to take their chances and return to more familiar ground, hoping to hide out along the Maroni River until a new escape could be planned.

During their march back, two of the men lagged behind, and later, only one caught up to the group, explaining that the other man had disappeared. The disappeared man's body was soon found — he had been murdered by his starving companion for his can of condensed milk. The murderer was then punished for his crime: he was killed by another of the group. By this time, the remaining six men were famished. They agreed to roast and eat the dead man's foot. Then, finding the foot edible, they butchered the rest of his body and ate that too. Belbenoit, alarmed by this turn to cannibalism, went along with the group's decision rather than risk their anger and possible repercussions. He had only been a hapless thief, but the others were murderers and hardened criminals; Belbenoit had learned how to survive among them.

After two more days, they reached an Indian village on the banks of the Maroni River where they were given dried fish and bananas. They began to doze after filling their empty stomachs, but were soon awakened by the sounds of men approaching. It was the Dutch police, alerted by the Indians that convicts had arrived in their village. The escape had failed, and they were soon back in the blockhouse at Saint Laurent.

One of Belbenoit's accomplices soon died of gangrene, a complication from the infections that developed in his feet during the escape attempt. The others remained in the fetid jail. Belbenoit became extremely ill and unable to eat. He was near death when he was finally allowed to go to the hospital. After recuperating, he had to face a trial for his second escape attempt. All prisoners who had broken any rules had to appear before the Tribunal Maritime Spécial, the presiding court for convicts. The trials were routine and the punishments regulated. For such crimes as stealing, fighting, injuring, verbal insults, and refusal to work, the punishment was one month to five extra years in prison. For more serious crimes such as murder or striking a guard, the punishment was six months to five years in solitary confinement — or the death penalty. (There was a guillotine on Île Royale in the prison courtyard.) For attempting to escape, the punishment was one to five years in solitary confinement for those with a life sentence, and from six months to three years in solitary for all others. Partly because of his poor health and his military service, Belbenoit received a sentence of six months in a labor camp along with the dreaded classification of "incorrigible."

He had been in French Guiana for two years.

⁓

Belbenoit was sent to the very worst of the colony's prison camps, Camp Charvein. Deep in the jungle, it was a malarial swamp. The convicts were forced to work all day long chopping down trees where they were allowed to wear only straw hats — they had no clothes — and this time Belbenoit was assigned to fell trees, not make hats. He filed a protest against his being deemed "incorrigible" — the rules stated that it took three escape attempts to be so classified, and since Belbenoit had only two, a new prison director accepted his petition. His request was granted within two months, and he was sent from the labor camp to the solitary confinement prison on St. Joseph Island. This might not seem like an improvement, but it was, for spending countless hours alone in a dank cell was better than having to work endless hours unclothed in the malarial jungle under a burning sun. St. Joseph would be Belbenoit's first experience of the Salvation Islands. "Life on the Islands […] was entirely different from the routine of the mainland prisons and camps. On the Islands, there is no work: On them, there is only punishment and waiting, great suffering and great restlessness."

Before Belbenoit could be sent into solitary confinement, he had to be treated at the hospital on Île Royale for his high fever and incessant vomiting. Belbenoit, at five feet, five inches tall and with a jockey's build, was naturally slight, but his weight nevertheless dropped to a skeletal 80 pounds. He was near death when a newly arrived doctor was able to treat his symptoms and save his life. He remained in the hospital for nearly six months, the term of his sentence, and he was allowed to leave the hospital without going to St. Joseph. Instead, he entered the Crimson Barrack on Île Royale.

The Crimson Barrack (*La Case Rouge*), so named for its bloody reputation, was the most dangerous in the entire penal colony; only the most violent criminals were sent there. Between 40 and 60 men were locked in a barrack 40 yards long by 6 yards wide. They slept in hammocks. Gambling and sex, the only diversions, often resulted in fights, stabbings, and murders. With these looming threats, a prisoner kept his money, tobacco, and contraband in a "plan," a metal suppository. Paid informers kept the commander of the prison up to date on any surreptitious schemes. No one could be trusted.

Belbenoit, tired of wearing rags, wrote to the head warden about his lack of clothing, and finally received a change of clothes. He also requested an office job to fight the monotony of island prison life. He was assigned a bookkeeping job keeping track of the prison's food supply. This job afforded him unheard of liberties, like access to pen and paper, and the ability to walk freely from his barracks to his job. As long as he returned to his barracks by 9 p.m., he was left alone.

One day a guard offered him a job as a tutor to his 16-year-old daughter who was soon to leave for school in Cayenne, but before she left, her father wanted her to have extra lessons. Belbenoit, who had a flair for writing and drawing, accepted. He was 27. They began an affair, meeting after sunset. Late one night, after overhearing a couple whispering in the shadows near the barracks, the guard caught sight of his daughter running home, and discovered that Belbenoit was the last man to enter the barracks. The next day, Belbenoit was sent to St. Joseph. "The Island of St. Joseph! The loathsome, the cursed and detestable! It is a place of punishment and repression unparalleled on earth for inflicting pain and slow death. It is here that the convict suffers most."

The three solitary confinement units on St. Joseph were built of cement, each with 48 cells. Along the roof ran an iron walkway where guards patrolled night and day. Each cell had an iron grill as a roof, making it possible for guards to watch down on everything going on inside the cell, and above that was a tin corrugated roof that blocked out the sunlight and some of the rain. Each cell, 12 by 9 feet, with 9-foot-high walls, was furnished with only a wooden bench and a bucket. Prisoners were allowed outside one hour a day. "The rest of the day he lives in a dim light; from dark to dawn — blackness and silence. His is alive in a tomb."

There were no books, no writing material, and nothing to do. Many prisoners went insane. Belbenoit was sentenced to 90 days in solitary. He had some tobacco and matches in his "plan," along with a few francs. He was able to bribe a guard to bring him some coffee and bananas. He spent his time pacing, repeating his steps over and over — prisoners racked up thousands of such miles. By standing on his bench, he could just reach the bars above the cell to do pull-ups. A guard caught him exercising, and he was sentenced to 45 extra days. He couldn't take it, he needed to get out. With his last francs, he bribed a guard to bring him a small amount of sulphuric acid from the infirmary. By breathing the fumes, he became sick, coughing severely enough to be sent to the hospital on Île Royale.

Belbenoit was able to complete his sentence in the hospital, and in February 1927, he was sent back to Saint Laurent on the mainland where he began another job as a bookkeeper. He started planning his next escape. Belbenoit learned that an American couple was visiting the prison colony and that they were taking photographs. Figuring that they were from a newspaper, he wondered if they might be interested in some of his prison experiences; he had been able to write them down on the scraps of paper he had salvaged from his desk job.

The couple, Robert and Blair Niles, were travel writers; they paid Belbenoit 100 francs for his notes. This was an enormous sum for a convict, and the next day, Mrs. Niles gave him 100 more for answering her questions. Over several days, these visits continued, until the Nileses were set to leave. Belbenoit saw the chance for an escape. With his newly earned money, he bought fresh clothes and tried to meet up with Mrs. Niles on her way to the departing ship in the hopes that she would help him, but the plan failed when Belbenoit was spotted by policemen. He was sent back to the Crimson Barrack, but he was able, by paying off a guard, to send more of his accounts to Mrs. Niles in New York. Based on Belbenoit's stories, she published her best-selling novel *Condemned to Devil's Island* in 1928; the film based on it, simply titled *Condemned*, was an early "talkie" and it came out the following year, premiering in Hollywood at Grauman's Chinese Theatre on December 5, 1929. The film was immediately attacked for being inauthentic. No one could believe that such a brutal place existed.

Belbenoit was able to continue writing in secret, sending a manuscript detailing the horrors of prison to the governor of the colony. As a result, during an inspection tour of Île Royale, the governor asked to meet with Belbenoit, and promised that if Belbenoit could go three months without any infractions, he would lift his "incorrigible" classification and send him from the islands to the mainland.

Belbenoit complied, and in November 1927, he was transported to Cayenne, his first time in the capital. "To see Cayenne is to see the depths of human degeneration…Today, ruined, French Guiana is the camping ground of futility." Nevertheless, all convicts hoped to be in the Cayenne prison as it was the least abusive in the colony, and convicts were permitted to work, albeit as slave labor, for local residents. They were also allowed to walk through the town on their way back to their barracks after completing their assignments.

A few months after he arrived in Cayenne, in February 1928, Belbenoit received a letter from Blair Niles advising him to serve out the remaining 18 months of his sentence without attempting to escape. But because of his eight-year sentence and the law of *doublage*, he would have to remain in the colony even if he was released, so he planned another escape, this time, via Brazil. With the money he had earned from Mrs. Niles, he bought new clothes, and importantly, a forged Brazilian passport along with papers proving he was not a convict, as well as a boat ticket to Saint Georges on the Brazilian border. Slipping away from his work gang, Belbenoit changed clothes and boarded the ship under his forged identity, Gabriel Ormières. (Ormières was the man who sold him the papers and himself an ex-convict.) Just as the boat was about to depart, a gendarme rushed up the gangplank, and Belbenoit, fearing trouble, walked off the ship and headed down the pier towards town, figuring he could slip back into the barracks. The gendarme caught up with him, demanding his papers. They appeared to be in order, except for one thing: the gendarme realized that the man in front of him could not be Gabriel Ormières — he had arrested him the night before. He ordered Belbenoit to accompany him to the police station to sort things out. It happened that Ormières, drunk from the rum he had purchased with his profits from the forged papers, had insulted the gendarme and was thrown in jail. Reading the passenger list, the gendarme saw Ormières's name and thought he was attempting to leave the colony, which was prohibited. Had Ormières not insulted the guard, Belbenoit would have sailed off to Brazil. Instead, his best chance of escaping came to a quick end, and with it, the certainty of extreme punishment for the attempt.

In November 1928, Belbenoit came before the court to learn his sentence. He received six months of solitary on St. Joseph, a much lighter punishment than he was expecting. He vowed to behave in an exemplary manner. After a few weeks, the commandant asked to speak with Belbenoit in his office on Île Royale. He had heard about Belbenoit's writing and wanted to read it. Having already sent it off to the governor, Belbenoit said he could re-write it, and the commandant ordered him to begin work at once. Paper and pen would be provided to him in his cell on St. Joseph. Belbenoit began to write, and in a short time, he was ordered to return to Cayenne where he was called into the governor's office. The governor had taken an interest in Belbenoit's work and was a more progressive official than had ever been in charge of the colony; he was interested in reform. Belbenoit had 10 months left of his sentence, and the governor offered him a deal: if Belbenoit promised not to try to escape, he could work on a boat that was mapping the coast. He agreed, and when several other convicts on the boat spotted a chance to escape, Belbenoit refused, honoring his promise.

For this, he was rewarded with a new and interesting job, that of cataloguing and organizing the colonial archives. They were in disarray as no one had ever bothered to put them in order — French Guiana once again defied Enlightenment rationality. The task of organizing and preserving France's historical archives had been decreed by the Revolutionary government in the 1790s when the Archives Nationales was founded, but the sensibility of such a plan never made it to the chaos that was French Guiana. For Belbenoit, this was a plum job, a chance to read over the entire history of the colony and gather extensive information for his planned exposé.

Near the end of his sentence, Belbenoit was asked by the governor what he planned to do once he was released. He replied honestly, saying that he would try to escape. The governor surprised him by offering to issue Belbenoit a passport so that he could leave the colony for one year in order to earn enough money to set himself up as an ex-convict upon his return. No such thing had ever been done, and Belbenoit could not believe that at last, his nightmare might cease.

But suddenly, he was removed from his job in the archives and given a new task, as a bookkeeper at the barracks. Others in the penal administration feared that with his access to the colony's records, Belbenoit would contact the writers he knew in the United States and that France's reputation would suffer. Although he was angry about losing his job, the position as bookkeeper had its advantages, for he could see which guards were siphoning off money; as a result, they gave Belbenoit a great deal of latitude. He spent his last days as a convict in relative calm, and finally, the day of his liberation arrived.

⁓

On September 21, 1930, Belbenoit was released from prison, given 85 francs (about $4), and told he would have to remain in French Guiana for the rest of his life — and that for 10 years, he would not be permitted within the city limits of Cayenne. He went immediately to see the governor.

True to his word, the governor signed a decree permitting Belbenoit to leave the colony for one year. He would be free to work and save up some money, and upon the advice of Mrs.

Niles, he decided to go to Panama. Within a week, he was off, the only liberated prisoner ever allowed to leave Devil's Island.

"I walked down the gangplank at Cristobal Colon, at the Atlantic entrance to the Panama Canal, and hastened to the French quarter where I secured a cheap room. Then I went out job hunting." For eight months, Belbenoit worked as a gardener at a hospital. His year of freedom was nearly over, and he wrote to the governor requesting that he be granted permanent freedom, only to learn that the governor had left the colony after his two-year term, replaced by another. Time was running out. He was due back on November 12, 1931.

Belbenoit decided to take a chance and appeal his case in France. He booked passage and arrived back in France on November 2. He had broken the law, and was immediately placed under arrest, spending two months in jail in Le Havre. He was then transferred to the prison at Île de Ré, the embarkation point for deported convicts, where he spent eight months in solitary confinement. He was then shipped back to French Guiana, arriving on October 7, 1932. It was as if he never left. He vowed that he would escape for good or die trying.

He was sentenced to solitary confinement on the islands, where he forced himself to endure the brutal treatment. "Day after day I fought there alone just to keep from rotting, rotting in mind and body." Finally, on November 3, 1934, he was freed, allowed to return to the mainland where he would begin his life as a "free convict."

Since he was barred from working, there was very little for him to do; he would have to rely on his own ingenuity. There were only two legitimate ways for a *libéré* to survive: catching butterflies in the jungle and selling them to dealers, or making handcrafted articles for tourists that were sold in French colonial hotels. Butterflies and trinkets paid very little, and only a meager living could be made, at best.

Nevertheless, Belbenoit began catching butterflies and managed to eke out an existence for a time, but he needed cash to fund another escape, and he had very little of it. A bit of luck soon came his way. One day he spotted a tourist, easily distinguished by his fresh clothes and pith helmet. The man asked if Belbenoit spoke English, and thinking he could earn a tip, he said he did even though his English was rudimentary. The man offered $5 to be taken to a convict named Belbenoit, the one Blair Niles had written about. Astonished, Belbenoit took the money and announced, "I am Belbenoit!" The man was a movie producer doing research. He paid Belbenoit $200 for information and left the next day. It was enough money to plan his fifth escape.

He needed to find at least five other *libérés* in order to have enough men to sail a boat, and one had to have navigational skills. He had in mind a route that would take them to Trinidad, a British colony and hence, safe — and from there, to Miami and ultimately, New York. He found five ex-convicts, among them, two robbers, a pimp, and two murderers. One of them had been a sailor and knew enough about navigation to guide them across the Caribbean.

They were able to buy a *cayuco*, an Indian canoe, from a local Chinese merchant, but when they went to retrieve it, it was only half the size they had agreed upon, and the provisions they had ordered were similarly halved. Nevertheless, they set off from Saint Laurent during the night of May 2, 1935. "Men in their right senses would never have gone out on the merciless Caribbean Sea in such a craft — but we were driven by a quite insane desire to put Devil's Island and the Penal Colony behind us—to seek freedom at any price." They were far out at sea by the next day, and they began rationing their food. A storm arose, but they were able to sail through it. By the third night, cramped in the small canoe, the men began to suffer the effects of sun, salt, and irritation with each other. When their keg of fresh water was ruined by sea water, they began to worry. "The fourth night was increasingly cruel. The fifth, sixth, seventh, eighth nights were nightmares, we became like six beasts. Eight more days we lived — how I do not know." Two of his companions began to doubt that they would ever reach Trinidad and argued that they should head back to the mainland. Belbenoit drew a small pistol, aiming it at them while insisting they stay their course. A fight broke out, and one of the "mutineers" was tied up so that his movements would not capsize the boat. At that moment, they spied land. They had reached Trinidad. The quarrelling stopped. Belbenoit threw his pistol into the sea.

It had taken 14 days to travel over 700 miles. The exhausted men landed on a beach where some fisherman gave them coconuts to quench their thirst and hunger, after which they reached a deserted hut where they found food and slept. Belbenoit advised the group that they should contact the authorities immediately, and after some resistance, the men followed his plan. They reached a small town and went immediately to the police station, where they were relieved to learn that not only would they not be deported, they would be fed and transported to Port of Spain, the capital. Upon reaching that city, they were taken to the headquarters of the Salvation Army, where they would stay until their future could be decided. One of the men obtained a forged Venezuelan passport and booked passage back to Europe; he had 4,000 francs in his "plan." The others contacted friends who might send them money, but they waited in vain.

While waiting, news of their arrival had spread, and several reporters and photographers went to see them. Among them was William LaVarre, an American explorer and adventurer who had made a fortune by discovering diamonds in British Guiana. LaVarre took an interest in Belbenoit, offering to safeguard his manuscript, but Belbenoit refused. (LaVarre was able to take photographs of the men which ultimately appeared in an article about their escape *in Life Magazine* on April 4, 1938.) Finally, the authorities in Trinidad offered to give the men a boat and provisions so that they could continue their voyage to the United States.

—————

They set out for Miami on June 10, 1935, knowing that at all costs, they had to avoid the French islands of Martinique and Guadeloupe. Hoping to reach Grenada, they became lost and spent six days sailing without knowing where they were. Six more days passed without sight of land. On the 13th day, they spotted a ship, and signaling to it, the ship approached them. It was German, and upon speaking to the captain, Belbenoit learned that they were 200 miles north of the Dutch colony of Curaçao, and that rather than sailing northwest, they had headed almost due west. There was very little chance of reaching Miami. The captain offered to take the men to Curaçao, but they refused, fearing that the Dutch would deport them back to French Guiana. Given supplies by the captain, they decided instead to head west to Panama, where, in the American zone, they would be safe. Sixteen days later they spotted land, and in attempting to land on the beach, their boat was smashed by the waves. Soggy but safe, they made their way onto land, where a group of Indians armed with spears met them. The Indians stole all their goods, including blankets, lamps, food, and clothing. The only thing Belbenoit was able to save was his manuscript — all his notes from Devil's Island. He had secreted it in an oilcloth pack, and it was of no interest to the Indians. The only other thing they were able to salvage was a machete undetected by the Indians. They had landed not in Panama, but on the northernmost point of Columbia, Punta Gallinas.

Naked and hungry, they were able to catch and eat a few fish, lizards, and frogs. Finally, on the third day, they came to a hut where they found some women's clothing. "Soon we all wore petticoats. With our bearded faces we were an astounding sight. But, clothed at last, we found that the insects didn't bother us so much."

Spending the night in an empty hut, the men were awakened by soldiers who burst out laughing upon seeing the rough-looking men in dresses. They were taken to the town of Barranquilla, given some old military uniforms, and told they would be turned over to the French Consul. Their tribulations had been in vain. They were put in jail, awaiting the next French vessel that would return them to Devil's Island. It was due in a month.

News of the arrival of Devil's Island convicts spread, and a newspaper editor came to visit Belbenoit. He wanted articles for his paper, and offered to pay Belbenoit for them. Not only that, he arranged for Belbenoit to escape. Bribing guards wasn't difficult. That night, Belbenoit heard the lock on his cell door open, and he made a dash for freedom into the streets of Barranquilla. He knew he had to reach Panama as soon as possible, and was able to hitch a ride to Cartagena. He didn't have enough money to pay someone to smuggle him on board a ship bound for Panama, so he decided to go on foot. But before he set out, he needed to obtain some cash, and he remembered that another escapee, Charlot Gautier, was living in the area, making a living catching and selling Blue Morpho butterflies, among the largest and most beautiful in the world. Gautier was more than surprised when Belbenoit knocked on his door, but he offered to help him, and after four months, Belbenoit had earned $100, enough to get him to Panama.

Before leaving, he read a newspaper account of his Barranquilla escape, learning that his comrades had all been deported back to Devil's Island, including the one with the forged Venezuelan passport, who had tried to enter France, was arrested, and like the others, sent back to the dry guillotine. Belbenoit alone had escaped.

Now all he had to do was walk to the Canal Zone through the Darién Gap, one of the most impenetrable jungles in the world; it remains the only break in the 16,000-mile long Pan American Highway. Very few white people have ever successfully traversed its swamps, sinkholes, jungles, steep mountains, and rushing rivers. The first post-colonial expedition through its confounding density was sponsored by the Smithsonian in 1924-25, and several adventurers have made the journey on foot over the decades, but such treks are rare and of course, the participants had ample provisions.

Belbenoit crossed the jungle alone, and with nothing more than a few supplies hastily stuffed into a backpack.

He set out, and after five days, came upon some Indians. Able to communicate in Spanish, Belbenoit learned that he would not be permitted to continue. The jungle was closed to white men. He told them he was there to catch butterflies, and that he could pay two pesos for any Blue Morphos. The Indians became interested, having never encountered such a project,

RENÉ BELBENOIT, AP WIRE PHOTO, 1938

but upon arriving, learned that the man was away. His servant let Belbenoit spend the night there, and advised him to retreat to his employer's banana plantation in the jungle in order to rest and recuperate from his harrowing voyage.

He took the advice, arriving at the secluded banana grove in two days, but its rough laborers, who only seemed interested in drinking and fighting, reminded him of the prison colony he had fled. He noticed some Indians, and began speaking to them. Their soft voices and quiet intensity intrigued him, and when he learned that there were enormous butterflies in the jungle where they lived, he asked if he could live with them. They agreed. "Thus began for me a seven-month adventure of sheer tranquility, peace, and I suppose you could even call it happiness."

Belbenoit began living among the Kuna Indians, following their customs and agreeing to their rules. He was not allowed to enter the jungle alone, he could not dig for gold, he could not bathe in the river at the same time as the villagers, and if he planned to stay for more than two months, he had to take a wife. (Single men were untrustworthy.) He accepted. The village chief chose a young woman who became Belbenoit's wife, Rachi-ti, The Flower-that-Sleeps. Belbenoit was given the name Nikat-chipu — which he translated as both White Man and The Man Who Catches Butterflies. At first, he could only communicate in an improvised sign language, but eventually, Belbenoit learned to speak Rachi-ti's language.

Months passed, and Belbenoit wondered if he would, or should, return to the outside world. During that time, the explorer LaVarre, whom he had met in Trinidad, was in the Panamanian jungle where he happened to come upon Belbenoit, who was

and invited Belbenoit to stay in their village for the night. But before dawn, Belbenoit crept out of the village, went down to the shore and stole one of the village canoes. He sailed all night, hiding during the day to avoid detection. After a few days, another group of Indians spotted him and took him to their village after he once again claimed to be a butterfly hunter — and again, he stole a canoe at night. He repeated this scenario for over 20 days before he finally reached his destination, the Caribbean side of the Panama Canal. He had traversed the Darién Gap. He swam ashore at Colon, taking with him only his manuscript.

He made his way to the French quarter of the city, where, mistaken for a local drunkard, he was given food, coffee, and fresh clothes. Sympathetic compatriots gave him money, and he was able to reach Panama City on the Pacific side. He had the address of a writer who he thought would be of help, on a butterfly hunt. Belbenoit took him to his jungle hut — which LaVarre photographed — and again, LaVarre offered to transport the escapee's manuscript to safety. Belbenoit again refused, but promised that if he was caught and sent back to Devil's Island, he would send it to LaVarre — and then kill himself. Soon after, when his desire for justice and his intent to report on the barbaric French penal system became paramount, Belbenoit did decide to leave his jungle sanctuary in order to find another in the United States.

After a four-day trek, he arrived back in Panama City. He sold his butterflies to Jungle Jim Price, who ran a curio shop, and headed northwest towards Costa Rica by truck. Near the border, he was arrested by guards who mistook him for a smuggler, but the official in charge let him go. He was able to stow away on a ship, making his way into Nicaragua, where he encountered bandits who stole all his money. He reached Managua where he was able to send an urgent telegram to Price, the butterfly dealer in Panama City, who sent him $50. He then entered Honduras by train, cleverly avoiding the police, and from there, he entered El Salvador, where he was warned not to try to cross into Guatemala — agents of its repressive dictatorship would certainly give him trouble. He had to find a way around Guatemala and enter Mexico, knowing that from there, he could travel safely into the U.S. .

On June 4, he managed to reach La Libertad, one of El Salvador's port cities, where he saw a Canadian-bound freighter loading cargo. He stowed away, hiding in a dark storage room. He had a few cans of sardines and little else. Twice he snuck on deck at night where he found the food of the ship's dog, which he ate, along with the dog's water, which he drank. After seven days, the ship made port. Belbenoit had carefully stowed his clothes so that they would remain clean, and he put them on. With a tiny razor, he shaved his beard. He went on deck. "Great rocky mountains of a yellowish color were piled up into magnificent shapes . . . I noticed that the guards only questioned the sailors and frisked them. They didn't ask anyone for identifying papers."

He thought he had docked at a Mexican port. In a way, he had. He had arrived at El Pueblo de la Reina de Los Angeles.

———

It was June 11, 1937, 14 years after his arrival in French Guiana, but before he could settle down in Angeltown, Belbenoit had to complete his burning desire to tell the world about Devil's Island.

Within a month, he took a bus to New York to meet William LaVarre, who helped Belbenoit arrange with E. P. Dutton the publication of the manuscript that Belbenoit had so zealously guarded. *Dry Guillotine: Fifteen Years among the Living Dead* appeared in February 1938. LaVarre wrote the introduction. It created a sensation, and within six months, it had gone through 15 printings. The book was instrumental in closing down France's notorious prison colony, and it led to many reforms in the French penal system.

But Belbenoit was facing immigration problems, and without any papers, he was deported in 1940. He went back to Panama, then to Mexico. In 1941, he was arrested in Brownsville, Texas for having entered the country illegally — by swimming across the Rio Grande. He was sentenced to 15 months in prison. The best-selling author could not get a break from U.

S. immigration authorities. He served yet another jail term, and once freed in 1942, Belbenoit returned to Los Angeles, where he attempted to enlist in the army. Because of his age, he was refused.

His story had appeared in numerous newspapers, and as he was known to many in the Hollywood community, he was hired as a technical advisor on *Passage to Marseille* (1944) when it was in production at Warner Bros. Considered as a follow-up to *Casablanca*, it featured many of the same cast members (Humphrey Bogart, Claude Rains, Sydney Greenstreet, Peter Lorre), and the two films shared the same director, Michael Curtiz. The film tells the story of five convicts who have escaped from Devil's Island in order to return to France to fight the Nazis, a combination of Belbenoit's own life mixed in with war propaganda.

Belbenoit had also met Lee Gumpert, the widow of a prominent Los Angeles physician; they fell in love and were married in 1945. Lee's brother-in-law was Emil Gumpert, a prominent attorney who helped Belbenoit in his quest to become a U.S. citizen. He was determined to stay in Los Angeles. With help from Gumpert, other prominent attorneys, and some influential Hollywood producers, Belbenoit's application for citizenship was granted a decade later, on January 18, 1956. He had achieved his goal.

By the time Belbenoit arrived in Los Angeles, it had morphed from the fancifully eccentric city of De Rudio's time into the uncategorizable megalopolis of 1.5 million that was driving the world's dreams through the movies. Hollywood had given the city even more glamour than it had enjoyed as a flowery paradise, and Los Angeles looked good on film. Not only was it home to the movies, Los Angeles in the 1940s and '50s was the center of the expanding aviation and aerospace industries, and it was the city that spawned much of modern life: freeways, ranch houses, diet fads, self-improvement schemes, and always, real estate opportunities. The tourist attractions of old — Venice, Mt. Lowe, and the ostrich farm — had morphed into Disneyland. Los Angeles was still the place where untried and unheard of plans could succeed. It didn't change its character over the years; the only things that changed were dreams: they got bigger. And above all, Los Angeles wasn't snobby; it accepted all comers, even escaped convicts from the jungles of Devil's Island. After all, one had already arrived over 40 years earlier.

During the late 1940s, Belbenoit discovered the beauties of Lucerne Valley and the high desert north of Los Angeles, attracted, no doubt, to a climate antithetical to that of French Guiana. The dry, desert air must have been soothing to the man who had endured years of jungle dampness. A promotional brochure on the area stated: "Every day you live in Lucerne Valley is a day more glorious, more enchanting, more happy, than any preceding days. You will shout joyously to the world that at last an earthly paradise has been discovered." In 1951 Belbenoit moved to the earthly paradise of Lucerne Valley where he opened René's Ranch Store. The prisoner who spent years without proper clothing became the purveyor of dude ranch and cowboy gear.

Belbenoit's wife Lee and her son from her first marriage commuted between their apartment in West Hollywood and Belbenoit's place in Lucerne Valley, usually visiting him on the weekends. He spent much of his time writing and was still the subject of various articles and interviews. In 1955, an episode of the popular television program *This Is Your Life* was devoted to him.

On February 26, 1959, Belbenoit died of a heart attack in his little store. A sheriff's deputy, who happened to drop by to say hello, found his body. According to a friend, veteran Los Angeles newspaper reporter Matt Weinstock, Belbenoit had been working on a new book, *Anatomy of Justice*. From his little bit of paradise in the desert, he continued to write about the hell that was Devil's Island.

—•—

POSTSCRIPT:
Timeless Angels

The City of Angels, for all its heavenly surface appeal, has hidden aspects; it retains its mysteries and secrets within a reservoir of shrouded, untapped memories. Bubbling below the surface like the city's famous tar deposits are many tales of remarkable people who lived unusual lives — and so, Los Angeles has kept the secret of the two "devils," until now. They have blended into the historical haze that has blanketed the city like the smoky fog that has clouded its reputation for years.

Los Angeles does not rely on the past, but on constant reinvention; the past is of little value. New visions bulldoze old ones at a rapid pace. Nothing lasts for long, nor is it supposed to. That is part of the city's charm. Its acceptance of change is admirable in many ways: a certain open-mindedness and willingness to try new things have been the result. Hollywood has been proving that for a century, but the city was already a laboratory for invention and novelty before the ascendancy of the movies. "Why not?" should be the city's motto. Even shortening its name to an abbreviation is emblematic of this spirit. Los Angeles is the vanguard of the new and the now. Not the city that time forgot, Los Angeles is the city that forgets time.

And because it celebrates novelty of all kinds, Los Angeles has always welcomed exotic strangers. Charles De Rudio, a larger-than-life romantic hero, was exactly the sort of person that Los Angeles worshipped at the dawn of the 20th century. His story fit right in with the city's fictionalized version of itself. He was a man of his moment, the perfect combination of attributes for his time, and especially, his place. Similarly, René Belbenoit was precisely the man to exemplify his time, mid-20th century Los Angeles, a city where the dangers lurking in the darkness belied the tranquility of its sunny days — the city as seen in film noir.

Although accepted, Belbenoit found his first years in Los Angeles troublesome — the lingering effects of his past cast a shadow over his future — but once he overcame his difficult past, his life became an archetypal Los Angeles one, complete with cowboy boots and spurs.

For both men, the devils were gone, the past had ended — as only it could — in El Pueblo de la Reina de Los Angeles. The City of Angels. Angeltown. L.A. ⁄⁄

CONTRIBUTORS

VICTORIA DAILEY is a writer, curator and antiquarian bookseller. She lives in Los Angeles.

FADY JOUDAH won the Griffin International Poetry prize in 2013. *Textu* is his most recent poetry collection, composed in character count on cellphone, available from Copper Canyon Press.

BRUCE ROBBINS is Old Dominion Professor in the Humanities at Columbia University and the author of *Perpetual War: Cosmopolitanism from the Viewpoint of Violence* (2012), *Upward Mobility and the Common Good: Toward a Literary History of the Welfare State* (2010), *Feeling Global: Internationalism in Distress* (NYU, 1999), *Cosmopolitics: Thinking and Feeling beyond the Nation* (1998), *Secular Vocations: Intellectuals, Professionalism, Culture* (Verso, 1993), and other books.

SARAH BLAKE'S poetry has appeared or is forthcoming in the *Michigan Quarterly Review*, the *Los Angeles Review*, *FIELD*, *Sentence: A Journal of Prose Poetics*, and *The Threepenny Review*.

ANNALISA QUINN is a journalist and book blogger for NPR and has degrees in classics and English from Georgetown University.

DANIEL OLIVAS, is the author of six books including, most recently, the award winning novel, *The Book of Want*. He is the editor of the anthology, *Latinos in Lotusland*, which brings together 60 years of Los Angeles fiction by Latino writers. He is a frequent contributor to *LARB*, and by day, Olivas is a supervising deputy attorney general in the Public Rights Division of the California Department of Justice.

GEOFF NICHOLSON lives in Los Angeles. His most recent book is *Walking in Ruins*.

FRANCESCA LIA BLOCK is a Los Angeles writer of over 32 novels, including *Weetzie Bat*, *The Rose and the Beast*, *The Hanged Man*, *Wasteland*, *I Was a Teenage Fairy*, and *Pink Smog*. She has received numerous awards, including the prestigious Margaret A. Edwards Lifetime Achievement Award, and her work has been translated into many languages.

MICHAEL WOOD teaches at Princeton; he is the author, most recently, of *Yeats and Violence*. His other books include *Literature and the Taste of Knowledge*, *The Road to Delphi*, *Children of Silence*, and *America in the Movies*.

MICHAEL ROBBINS is the author of *Alien vs. Predator* (Penguin, 2012). His poems have appeared in *The New Yorker*, *Poetry*, *Harper's*, *Boston Review*, and elsewhere.

DINAH LENNEY is a writer and actor — she most recently played a nun with a gun on *Sons of Anarchy*. She is the author of *Bigger than Life: A Murder, a Memoir* and the co-author of *Acting for Young Actors*. She is on the core faculty at Bennington College, the Rainier Writing Workshop, and in the Master of Professional Writing program at USC. Her memoir, *The Object Parade*, is forthcoming from Counterpoint in spring 2014.

LEO BRAUDY is a professor of English, cultural history, and film studies at the University of Southern California. His most recent book is a memoir, *Trying to Be Cool: Based on a True Story*.

COLIN DICKEY is the author of *Cranioklepty: Grave Robbing and the Search for Genius*, and *Afterlives of the Saints: Stories from the Ends of Faith*. His work has also appeared in *Lapham's Quarterly*, *Cabinet*, *TriQuarterly*, and other places. He is the co-editor (with Nicole Antebi and Robby Herbst) of *Failure!*

GEORGE PROCHNIK is editor-at-large for *Cabinet* magazine. His new book, *The Impossible Exile*, a study of Stefan Zweig and the psychology of exile, will be published in May 2014.

LAUREN K. ALLEYNE is a native of Trinidad and Tobago. Her work has been awarded prizes such as the 2003 *Atlantic Monthly* Student Poetry Prize, the Robert Chasen Graduate Poetry Prize at Cornell, an International Publication Prize from *The Atlanta Review*, and honorable mention in the 2009 Reginald Shepherd Memorial Poetry Prize and the 2003 Gival Press Tri-Language Poetry Contest.

JACK PENDARVIS lives in Oxford, Mississippi. He is the staff writer for the television show *Adventure Time*.

M.P. RITGER is a lecturer in the English department at Cornell University. His poems have appeared or are forthcoming in *The Beloit Poetry Journal*, *The Seattle Review*, and the anthology *Best New Poets* (2011).

SUSAN STRAIGHT is the author of nine books of fiction, a finalist for the National Book Award and winner of the Milkweed National Fiction Prize. She teaches at UC Riverside.

ALICE BOLIN'S essays are featured in *The Paris Review Daily*, The *New Yorker*'s Page-Turner Blog, *PopMatters*, and *This Recording*. Her poetry has been published in *Guernica*, *Blackbird*, *Washington Square* and many other journals. She lives in California.

LAILA LALAMI is a Moroccan American novelist. She is a professor of creative writing at the University of California at Riverside and the author of the novels *Hope and Other Dangerous Pursuits*, *Secret Son*, and the forthcoming *The Moor's Account*.

JOHN RECHY was the first novelist to receive PEN Center USA's Lifetime Achievement Award, a recipient of the Bill Whitehead Award for Lifetime Achievement from Publishing Triangle, an NEA fellow, and the first recipient of and the first recipient of *ONE Magazine*'s Culture Hero Award. A pioneer of gay and Chicano literature, he is the author of 11 novels and two books of nonfiction. His groundbreaking *City of Night* was published this year in a 50th-anniversary edition.

NOVELS TO STIMULATE
THE INTELLECT AND THE IMAGINATION

CLOTH • 978-1-60598-478-0
368 pages • $25.95

THE WINDSOR FACTION
by D. J. Taylor

"A fascinating glimpse into a murky part of British history."

—*The Wall Street Journal*

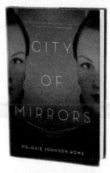

CLOTH • 978-1-60598-468-1
352 pages • $25.95

THE CITY OF MIRRORS
by Melodie Johnson Howe

"Deftly written, smart, [and] entertaining as hell."

—Michael Connelly

CLOTH • 978-1-60598-482-7
336 pages • $24.95

VINTAGE ATTRACTION
by Charles Blackstone

"If you like pugs, wine, and Greece, *Vintage Attraction* is for you. I loved every word."

—Gary Shytengart,
New York Times bestselling author
of *Super Sad True Love Story*

CLOTH • 978-1-60598-470-4
352 pages • $25.00

THE TRANSLATOR
by Nina Schuyler

"An elegant, poetic meditation on the art of translation."

—*Shelf Awareness*,
starred review

CLOTH • 978-1-60598-485-8
384 pages • $25.95

THE COLLECTOR OF LOST THINGS
by Jeremy Page

"Page writes with feeling and intimacy. His touch is poetic and sure."

—*The Guardian*

CLOTH • 978-1-60598-491-9
512 pages • $25.95

BYRON EASY
by Jude Cook

"Daring, moving, imaginative and, above all, funny."

—*The Sunday Mirror*

Pegasus Books
www.pegasusbooks.us

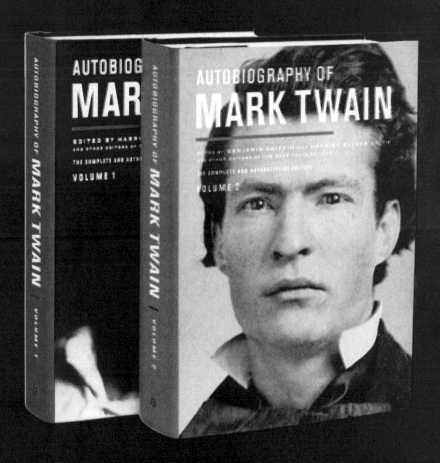

Jack Geary presents

Andy Hall

February 21 - March 30, 2014

185 Varick Street
New York NY